BOOKCASES

BOOKCASES

Outstanding Projects from America's Best Craftsmen

WITH PLANS AND COMPLETE INSTRUCTIONS
FOR BUILDING 11 CLASSIC BOOKCASES

NIALL BARRETT

The Taunton Press

Publisher: Jim Childs
Associate publisher: Helen Albert
Associate editor: Strother Purdy
Copy editor: Nancy Humes
Indexer: Peter Chapman
Cover designer: Steve Hughes
Interior designer: Lori Wendin
Layout artists: Susan Fazekas, Amy Bernard Russo
Front cover photographer: Chris Holden
Back cover photographers: Christian Becksvoort (top), Chris Holden (bottom)
Interior photographer: Chris Holden, except where noted
Illustrators: Bob La Pointe, Mark Sant'Angelo

Taunton
BOOKS & VIDEOS

for fellow enthusiasts

The Taunton Press, Inc.,
63 South Main Street, PO Box 5506, Newtown, CT 06470-5506
e-mail: tp@taunton.com

Distributed by Publishers Group West

Library of Congress Cataloging-in-Publication Data
Barrett, Niall.
    Bookcases : outstanding projects from America's best craftsmen / Niall Barrett.
        p.   cm. — (Step-by-step)
    Includes bibliographical references and index.
    ISBN 1-56158-303-0
    1. Bookcases—United States. 2. Cabinetwork. I. Title. II. Series: Step-by-Step
(Taunton Press)
    TT197.5.B6B37   1999
    684.1'6—dc21   99-15008
                                                    CIP

ABOUT YOUR SAFETY

Working with wood is inherently dangerous. Using hand or power tools improperly or ignoring standard safety practices can lead to permanent injury or even death. Don't try to perform operations you learn about here (or elsewhere) unless you're certain they are safe for you. If something about an operation doesn't feel right, don't do it. Look for another way. We want you to enjoy the craft, so please keep safety foremost in your mind whenever you're working with wood.

To Helle. "nobody, not even the rain, has such small hands."
—*e. e. cummings*

ACKNOWLEDGMENTS

I have come to realize that there is a veritable army of people who contributed their knowledge and efforts to producing this book, some of whom I have never met. I'd like to thank these individuals first, since I'm sure they're as proud of this work as I am.

I would especially like to thank the many talented craftspeople whose work inspired a number of the projects in this book: Christian Becksvoort, Curtis Erpelding, David Fay, Randy O'Donnell, Kevin Rodel, Lon Schleining, and Peter Turner. Their total unselfishness in freely sharing their work, insights, and experience lent this book the variety and clarity it would never have achieved alone. I hope I have done their work justice.

I would also like to thank Helen Albert for her accessibility and encouragement. All things have to start somewhere!

A special thanks to my editor Strother Purdy, who possessed the extraordinary amount of humor and patience it took to provide order in the chaos and keep me on track.

Thanks to my good friend and photographer (for this book) Chris Holden for his tireless efforts to create perfection under difficult circumstances and patience under my obsessive art direction. The results of his professionalism and attention to detail are apparent wherever one looks in this book!

I would also like to specifically thank Helene and Scott Harrison, along with all my other dedicated and incredibly patient clients who put aside their needs and rearranged their schedules so that this book wouldn't suffer.

A personal acknowledgment goes to Scott Gibson for his interest in glue and clocks!

Finally, I would like to express my appreciation to all the craftsmen who contributed their ideas and generously gave their time and knowledge, but weren't included in this book. Their contributions were nonetheless valuable.

CONTENTS

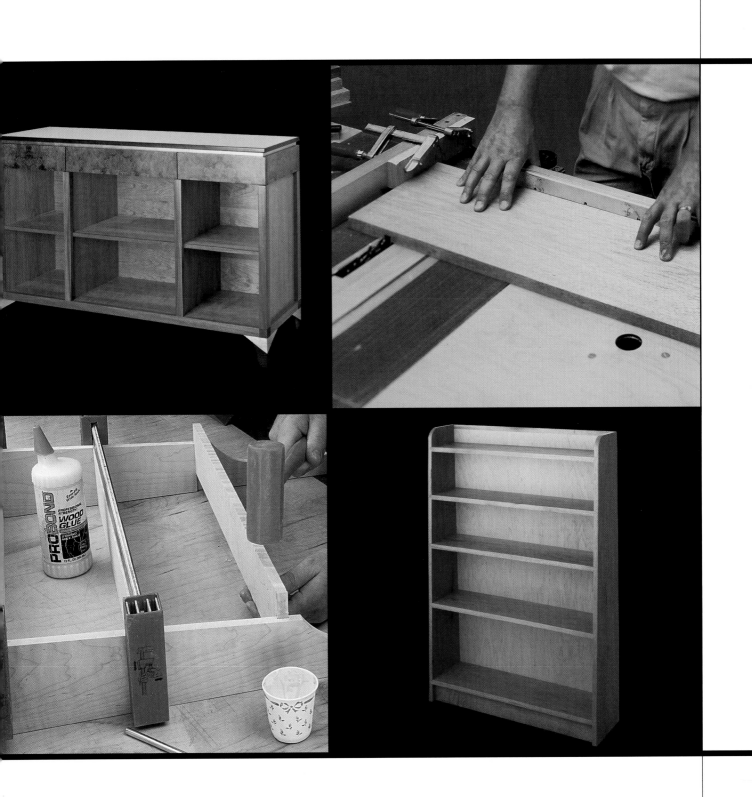

INTRODUCTION

I still remember my first paying job. It was building a bookcase, of course. I wasn't paid very much, but looking back, I was probably paid more than the job was worth. The clients were pleasant people and knew just what they wanted: a 2-ft.-high by 4-ft.-long plywood bookcase with fixed shelves to fit in an alcove under a window. I decided to build it with plain dadoes and screws since the alcove would hide the sides.

At first, I was relieved to get such a simple project. I was afraid of being asked to build something more complicated and not being able to say no. But what woodworker would be in over his head with a bookcase? The resulting comedy of errors is a good example of how lack of experience and knowledge of materials can end in a series of relatively small errors that will take you down dark alleys of frustration.

I learned that ¾-in. plywood is not really ¾ in. thick. Unfortunately, I discovered this after I cut the dadoes, so the joint was a tad loose. Not a problem, I said. The bookcase was being painted, so I would fill the joint.

All of this would have worked, I suppose, if the bookcase actually fit the space. Alcoves in old homes aren't square, and who knew I had to take into account the thickness of base molding? I should also tell you about the windowsill that was ½ in. lower on one side than the other (I only measured the height on one side apparently).

No problem, I said. I can learn from my mistakes. I built a new bookcase that fit the alcove nicely, with only minor persuasion. I congratulated myself on getting through the job, collected my check, and went home.

A couple of weeks later, after the painting and decorating were finished, my clients called to say that the case was not quite deep enough and that their books overhung the front. After some fast thinking, I made the point that the depth of the alcove determined the bookcase depth, over which I had no control. They agreed, and life went on.

A month or so later I was back on site trying to explain why there was a very noticeable sag in the shelves. Obviously they needed intermediate support. I installed center dividers, the painter came back, and once again life went on.

Building that bookcase taught me to research jobs carefully before I begin them, a practice I continue to this day. This book brings together all the information you'll need to build freestanding bookcases. In the first chapter I show the basic options, choices, and limits that are important to design and build a good bookcase. The heart of the book is 11 projects that reflect the essence of a self-contained bookcase. Collected from across America, the projects range from easy to medium in difficulty, and cover as many designs and styles. They're all examples of good design and construction that will prove useful to you for future projects.

This book won't guarantee a mistake-free career, but it should help you build confidence and allow you to concentrate on the enjoyable aspects of furniture building and design. So have fun!

BOOKCASE-BUILDING BASICS

AT HEART, BOOKCASES are simply open shelf storage that keep whatever we want within easy reach. They received their association with books, and consequently their name, a long time ago; but now people put fewer books in bookcases. The objects they now house range from the traditional books of all sizes, magazines, photo albums, and ring binders to more modern media such as CDs, VHS tapes, and the electronic equipment that plays them. Bookcases also do the job of display cases, housing art objects, pottery, and even a collection of antique radios. In short, they store anything and everything that we want within easy reach.

Good bookcases are first and foremost storage containers and should be designed around the objects they hold. Bookcases should both display and keep their contents out of harm's way. These requirements often lead to an open architecture, where one or more sides are open and do not have structural elements. This presents a challenge to make them strong. To solve these issues and others, this chapter will give you basic information to help you learn the essential requirements of a good bookcase, which you can use to design and build your own, as well as the projects offered later in the book.

PARTS OF A BOOKCASE

The basic requirements of a bookcase can be broken down by its parts and the jobs they do (or should do).

Base

The base of a bookcase is its anchor, both structurally and visually. It must offer the bookcase a firm footing and be large enough to support the often-considerable weight of what is stored in the bookcase. Freestanding bookcases should be sturdy enough to resist toppling if someone accidentally falls against them.

Bases shouldn't look clunky or out of proportion to the rest of the piece. When designing a bookcase, keep the proportions of furniture you like in mind, and draw your ideas first before committing them to wood. Always sleep on a new design.

Good bases can range from the continuation of the sides past the bottom shelf to a complex assembly of molding with separate feet. Their primary function, to give stability and strength, can be obtained without too much fuss. Everything else is looks, and the most appropriate base for a given bookcase will probably be more a question of its style than its strength (see "Bookcase Base Options" on p. 6).

Sides

The sides, or uprights, most often have the lonely job of keeping the whole structure standing. They support the shelves and tie the top and base together. Rigidity and density are key here because the sides will carry the weight down to the base or floor. Rigidity and density come with the choice of materials, and their thickness and width. Sides can also get a lot of support from fixed shelves and a back.

Bookcases aren't just for books anymore. They are commonly used to house any number of items, such as a ceramics collection in this 18th-century-style bookcase.

The other important job the sides perform is supporting the shelves. They carry the shelf-support system, whether rabbets, shelf-pin holes, or shelf standards. A reasonably high-density material is important because most support systems exert high crushing stresses on the wood. Shelf pins in soft woods such as pine and poplar can support lightly loaded shelves, but will eventually pull free under heavy loads. This is less important if metal standards are used.

Shelves

Shelves perform the obvious task of keeping the contents level, stable, and orderly. Though shelves are often the easiest part to make, woodworkers most often go wrong here. This is evident each time you see a sagging shelf.

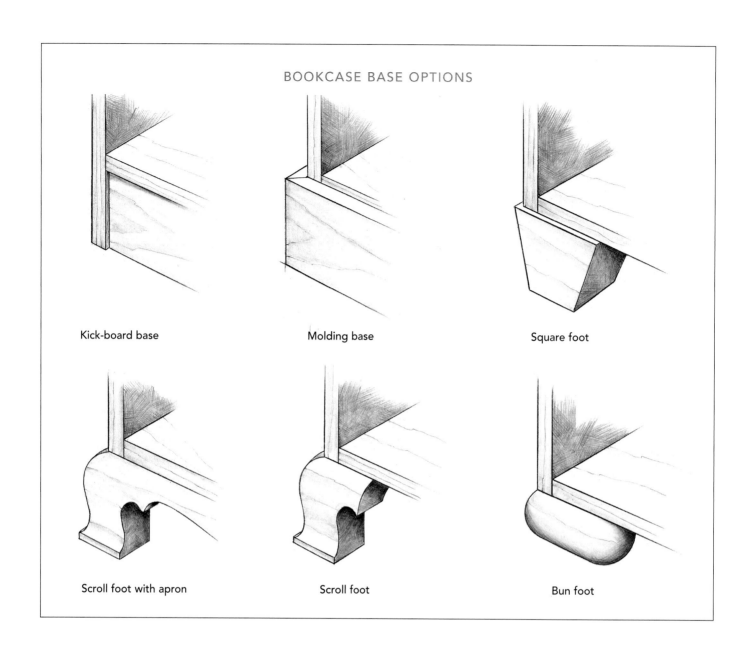

BOOKCASE BASE OPTIONS

Kick-board base

Molding base

Square foot

Scroll foot with apron

Scroll foot

Bun foot

As with the sides, rigidity is important for good shelves but even more so. High rigidity can be obtained through a combination of material choice and shelf design.

The most common materials used to make shelves are MDF (medium-density fiberboard), plywood, and solid wood (both hard and soft).

Medium-density fiberboard MDF does not get a lot of respect among custom furniture makers because it's mainly used in inexpensive production furniture. In the right situation, however, it's a very useful material, such as in paint-grade projects. Few materials give you as flat and smooth a surface as MDF. And when properly supported and veneered, using MDF can be a very economical way to produce a bookcase.

MDF is not the best shelving material choice for several reasons. It's extremely heavy, but has trouble supporting its own weight. All but the shortest spans must be supported. Unsupported spans longer than a couple of feet will sag noticeably under an average load of books. This also makes MDF a poor choice for structural members such as the bases and sides. MDF is also not very attractive.

Forty pounds is supported easily by a 60-in.-long span of ¾-in. oak (top shelf). However, ¾-in. hardwood plywood (next lower) can support only 25 pounds without sagging. The ¾-in.-thick pine shelf (next lower) doesn't do as well, but is better than the ¾-in. particle-board shelf (next lower). Finally, the ½-in. plywood shelf on the bottom really shows its inherent weakness.

Add strength to your shelves with a simple edge lip. Or build a torsion box with a lattice or honeycomb core for outstanding rigidity and strength.

Plywood Furniture-grade plywood is the modern shop workhorse: It can be used to build a wide range of projects. At least as strong as most softwoods, it is unaffected by seasonal humidity changes. Plywood can support an average weight of books over a 30-in. span, but not much more.

Plywood is commonly available in most North American hardwood species with a wide range of core options and can be special-ordered in just about any wood you can name (though not necessarily pronounce). There can be a size problem since you're generally limited to 96 in. with the grain and 48 in. across it. Solid wood does not have these size limitations. Special larger sheets of plywood can be ordered, but your wallet will wince. Most plywoods have an unattractive edge that should be covered by edgebanding of some kind.

Solid wood Solid wood is the choice for bookcases built with traditional joinery, espe-

cially exposed joinery. Dovetailed drawer boxes and finger-jointed cases in plywood are not unheard of, but they are the exception. Solid wood eliminates the need for edgebanding and also allows you to use thicker material to prevent shelves from bowing. A ¾-in.-thick shelf made of a softwood such as pine or butternut will also carry an average weight of books over a 30-in. unsupported span. In longer spans, sometimes all that's needed to eliminate sagging is ⅞-in. material instead of ¾-in. material.

Although there are considerable strength differences between hardwoods and softwoods, for most objects that bookcases hold, the choice between them is primarily aesthetic. On the other hand, I would question the use of even large thicknesses of a really soft wood in a bookcase that will be supporting extremely heavy objects.

Engineered shelves Shelves don't need to be flat boards. They can have lips on one

Fixed intermediate supports spread the load across these 48-in.-long shelves and keep them from sagging. (Photo by Joe Romero.)

Back

Bookcase backs can contribute tremendously to overall strength of construction. They can add great resistance to racking stresses, which otherwise would push the case out of square and into a parallelogram. Backs are not always welcome in a design, however, and a lot of bookcases are constructed without backs to achieve a certain look. Backless construction is possible but has size limits that require some other type of bracing, or the bookcase has to be fastened to the wall.

A well-fitted back can help square up the whole assembly, stiffen the sides, and resist racking. If you have to anchor the bookcase to the wall, a substantial back (at least $\frac{1}{2}$ in. thick) is invaluable. It will also allow you to screw the backs of fixed shelves directly through it to help support them.

There are several options for backs. Plywood is perhaps the most common, since its one-piece construction is labor saving and you don't have to worry about wood movement. To compensate for wood movement, solid-wood backs have to use tongue-and-groove boards or frame-and-panel assemblies, which can be quite complicated. These last options are certainly more attractive, although it could be argued that the back of a bookcase is rarely seen.

Top

The job of bookcase tops is to tie the sides together, much the way the base does on the bottom. Many bookcases, such as the short basic bookshelf on pp. 18-31, seem to lack a top, but they have one. Regardless of where the sides end, they have to be held together at or near the top. The top shelf or some elaborate assembly with crown molding can accomplish this. It may not be the most difficult job for a component, but you can't build a bookcase without it.

DESIGNING A CUSTOM BOOKCASE

A lot of bookcase projects start with a need to store something. But the questions involved quickly become concerned with the look,

edge or backbone strips along the middle of the underside. This structure gives thinner material much greater stiffness. Lips on both edges create half an I-beam, a very rigid construction. Other more complex options include veneered torsion boxes and honeycomb cores. These are very elegant solutions to the problem of shelf strength. A well-built $\frac{3}{4}$-in.-thick torsion box shelf can easily support books without sagging for 3 ft. to 4 ft., without additional supports. For all but the most heavy-duty applications or where you want unsupported spans longer than my standard 30 in., they are overkill. Another simpler way to make a plain shelf more rigid is to attach it to the back of the case or to intermediate supports.

Bookcase Back Options

When a bookcase needs a back, there are several options.

SHIPLAP

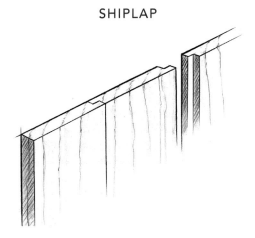

Wood movement is contained within the overlapping pieces.

TONGUE AND GROOVE

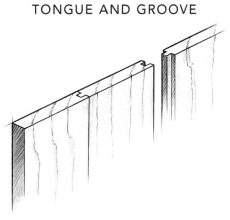

Wood movement is contained within the panels, which move freely in grooves.

PLYWOOD

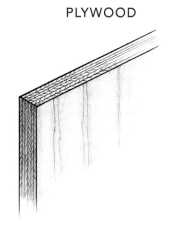

Stable, with no perceptible movement.

EDGE-GLUED SOLID WOOD

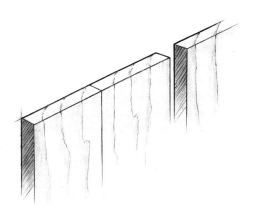

The wood has nowhere to move, so the back will buckle or break the case when expanding and crack or pull away from the case when shrinking.

FRAME AND PANEL

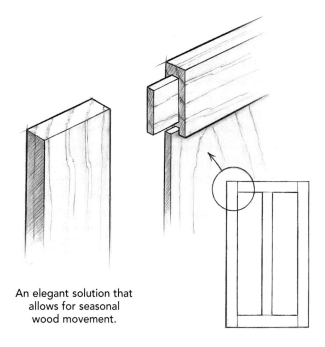

An elegant solution that allows for seasonal wood movement.

style, and how it will fit with the other furniture in the house. Though these questions are important, it's best to keep the original purpose of the bookshelf in mind, which is to store something.

In the initial design stages, there are a lot of considerations to juggle. They include the items the bookcase is to contain; its placement in the room; the size of the allotted space; and the maximum height, width, and depth. Maximum depth, for example, is a function not only of available space, but also of traffic patterns and the storage space required. It's no good designing a beautiful piece of furniture that sticks out so far that you have to turn sideways to pass it, or that isn't deep enough to hold the giant bowl that's the heart of the ceramics collection the case will house.

The size and weight of the objects also influence your choice of materials and joinery, not to mention whether the bookcase must have a back to be strong enough.

Start by taking an inventory of the items the bookcase is likely to store, and from there make a list of dimensions, including clearance and access space, and the approximate weight of the objects it will hold.

Sizes and weights of common objects

This is by no means a complete or definitive list, but it will give you an idea of what to look for and think about when you catalog all the items that need to be stored. Keep in mind that change is inevitable; a bookcase that

How tall are your favorite books? Be sure to design shelf heights tall enough to store what you want to put on them.

Books are heavy: Five books make a ¼-in.-thick shelf bow quite a bit, while a whole row of much lighter CDs doesn't make a similar shelf bow at all.

Drawers are more efficient for storing CDs than open shelves because they don't waste the height space.

houses a collection today might hold stuffed animals or possibly heavy books tomorrow.

Books Most hardcover books will fit on a 9-in.-deep shelf and in a 10-in. height, with a range of 8 in. to 10 in. deep and 8 in. to 10 in. between shelves (with more clearance for oversize books, art books, and law books). A good way to familiarize yourself with this range is to visit a bookstore with a tape measure in hand. You might get strange looks, but just inform the staff that you're measuring the books and they should leave you alone (just kidding). As a rule of thumb, remember that smaller items can go in taller shelves, but not the other way around.

Apart from dimensions, I can tell you that books are heavy. While softcover books can weigh as little as a few ounces, a row of hardcover novels can easily weigh a pound an inch. I have some art books that weight four times this amount. Over the span of a shelf, this adds up fast. Suffice it to say that weight is an issue with books, and they need relatively strong and rigid shelves to support them.

Electronic media CDs, audio tapes, and video tapes can be stored on open shelves, but there will be a lot of wasted space because they don't require very much depth or height. If you plan to put CDs on shelves, you should either design shallow shelves that won't be useful for holding much else, or have the CDs use up the space of normal-depth shelves, which is an inefficient use of space (and looks odd). For this reason it's best to store CDs and tapes in drawers located near their associated electronics.

A 6-in.-deep drawer will hold CDs, audio tapes, and video tapes, including their storage racks. The width and length will of course depend on which of these items or combinations of items you wish to store and the available space in the unit. I have also made some inserts that fit on the existing shelves and allow two rows of CDs to be stored one on top of the other. This still wastes a bit of depth on most bookcases, but it utilizes the height well and looks a lot better.

LPs (believe it or not, I am often asked to build bookcases around these for those collectors still out there) are a little more than 12 in.

Different objects demand different types of shelving and space allotments. Stereo equipment generally ends up at the bottom of a bookcase because it needs much greater shelf depth than do books, though it's not necessarily heavier.

DOVETAIL JOINT

Dovetails are an attractive and extremely strong choice for a corner joint between side and top or base. Use it when you need strength or want a traditional look. It's difficult to hand-cut and fussy to set up with dovetail jigs. And it loses both looks and strength if not well executed.

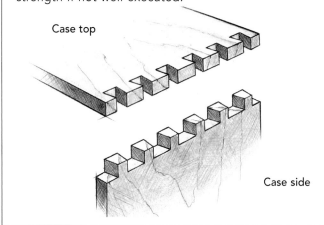

Case top

Case side

BOX JOINT

A very decorative corner joint, traditionally used for boxes (hence the name). When well executed it can be extremely strong and attractive, especially when the fingers are small.

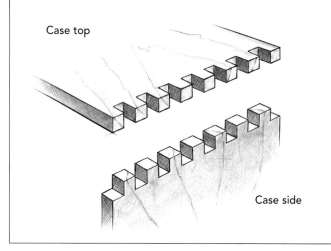

Case top

Case side

DOWELED JOINT

A tried-and-true method and still a good choice for both corners and shelving in medium-duty applications. Dowels are a hidden joint, so it's easy to hide errors. Accuracy of hole placement and size are fussy and critical for strength.

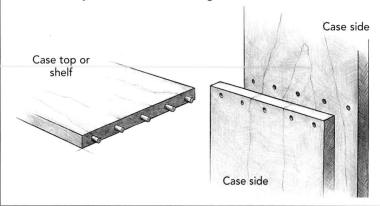

Case side

Case top or shelf

Case side

deep and need 12 in. to 13 in. of height. On an open 12-in. shelf they stick out just enough to make it easy to finger through them. Unlike CDs and video tapes, LPs weigh quite a bit per inch along a shelf—even more than books (try lifting a linear foot of LPs and you'll see what I mean). Be sure to build shelves strong enough to support them.

Home audio equipment was originally modeled after professional equipment, which was "rack-mounted." Rack-mounted equipment has mounting ears on each end of the face with holes for bolting them to a metal rack. The standard width for these racks, or more precisely the width between the mounting holes, is 19 in. Much home equipment is smaller, but 19 in. is still a good standard.

Audio equipment depths rarely exceed 16 in., but 2 in. to 3 in. extra for wires and plugs must be included. Access for power cables and interconnect cables to other components must also be considered. These add up quickly, which is why you most commonly see stereos in the deeper bases of bookcases, or in their own, much deeper entertainment centers.

I've left out a discussion of things like televisions, since I believe this is the role of the "wall unit" or the entertainment center. Stereo systems already push the envelope. It would be a very ungainly bookcase that could hold anything but the smallest of TVs, though there is talk of super-thin television sets around the corner.

BISCUIT JOINT

A relatively new technology, biscuits are excellent for just about any application where they will fit, from corners to fixed shelves to intermediate supports and dividers. They are a medium-duty joint, but the ease of alignment and fit make them almost foolproof.

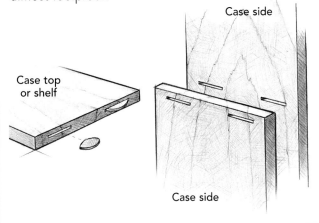

DADO AND RABBET JOINTS

The dado is a perfectly adequate joint for most shelving, with good shear strength. The rabbet is an open-sided dado and is good for joining the corners of a case. Both joints can look tidy but don't add much strength, so they need some other kind of attachment such as nails or screws.

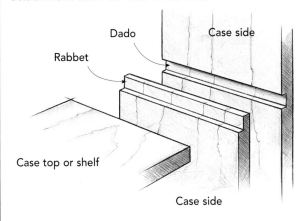

SLIDING DOVETAIL JOINT

An elegant and extremely strong way to connect a shelf. It can be fussy to cut and assemble, but with a good jig the work can go quickly. It loses both looks and strength if not well executed.

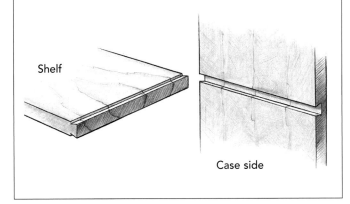

MORTISE-AND-TENON JOINT

A good choice for fixed shelves but not for corner joints. Aside from the through version shown, there are several other varieties, including a hidden stopped tenon(s) or stub tenon(s). Through tenons can be wedged.

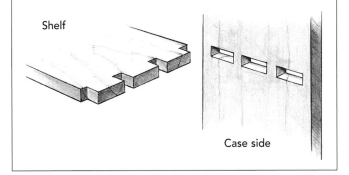

Joinery choices

Most well-executed joints are perfectly adequate for bookcase construction. Choosing among them is mostly a question of aesthetics, your skill level, and the machinery you have on hand.

I separate bookcase-construction joinery into two distinct areas: case joinery and shelf attachment. These certainly can and often do use the same joints, but it's a good exercise in construction logic to separate them because they have distinctly different forces acting on them.

The joinery connecting the sides, top, and base has to resist side-to-side racking. This job becomes especially difficult if there is no

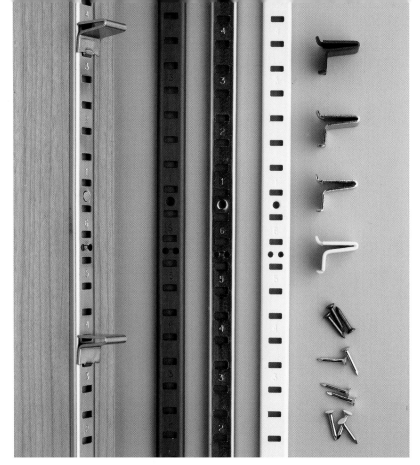

A shop-built notched-strip support system can be just the elegant detail to make your bookcase stand out from the others.

Commercial standards are very strong and relatively easy to install and can be a good choice for a simple project.

back to support the structure. The case also has to resist being pulled apart when being moved. Most captured joints such as dovetails and pegged mortises and tenons resist these forces well. Other good choices are dowels, box joints, and even biscuits.

On the other hand, the joints that connect the shelves to the sides have to resist extreme down or shear forces. These are very different forces to contend with. While most times shelf pins or fixed shelves with dowels or biscuits are adequate, in extreme cases there is no substitute for sliding dovetails or dadoes.

Hardware, jigs, and fasteners

Most bookcase hardware is associated with making the shelves adjustable. There are many more choices than can be covered here, but the ones listed work well, are easily obtained, and are representative of other available types. There are a few choices for non-commercial or shop-built adjustable shelf-support systems and jigs for line-boring as well as shelf-support pin options. A few of the projects in this book use hinges and drawer glides, but these are not specific to

bookcases and will be discussed in their respective chapters.

I have also included other types of fasteners such as screws and nails for two reasons. First, I felt I would be remiss if I didn't at least mention knockdown fasteners, since I use them quite a bit in my own furniture (see Step-Back Bookcase on pp. 162-181). Bookcases can often be large or tall enough to require breaking them down to move them. Second, Randy O'Donnell's bookcase on pp. 68-79 requires cut nails as part of its joinery and molding attachment. This was common practice in some period pieces, and even today it's not uncommon to use small brads to attach molding.

There is room for all these methods and countless more. If you think something will work, give it a try. A couple of nails or screws instead of hand-cut dovetails here or there can do wonders for your sanity (if nothing for the strength of the case).

Commercial standards Commercial shelf standards can be found in just about every hardware store in North America. They're strong enough for most applications, very easy to install, and just screw into the

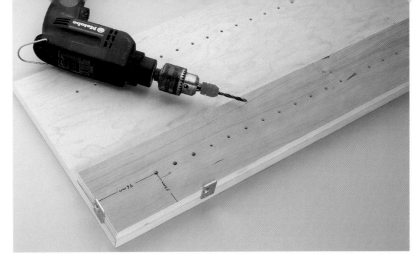

bookcase side. They come in a huge range of sizes, designs, colors, and finishes. Some are very basic shiny steel, while other "designer" standards have baked enamel finishes or brass plating and a lacquer finish. Frankly, I don't find any of them attractive or elegant. Because they stand proud from the bookcase sides, the shelf must either be notched around the standard or cut short enough to fit between. Nevertheless, for the quick, utilitarian projects we all have now and again, they have their place.

Shop-built shelf-support systems With a little looking around and/or some ingenuity, you can design and make your own shelf-support system. I've used a number of them over the years, from simple carved solid-wood pegs to the more elaborate, but still relatively easy, notched wood strips. There are a couple of advantages to making your own system. You can be sure that the support system integrates visually with the rest of the piece. It can also be just the thing to set apart your project from the crowd. However, as it adds time and fuss to a project, reserve a unique system for very special bookcase projects.

Line-boring and shelf pins The method I use most often for adjustable shelves is line-boring with shelf pins. It's very discreet, reasonably elegant, and there are endless pin options for a wide variety of special applications such as glass shelves. Of the several different types of shelf pins available, the most common fit is either 5mm or ¼-in. holes. Some also use sleeves that fit into a hole, then a pin fits into the sleeve. These are typically used in heavy-duty applications but are sometimes chosen for their appearance. In any case, choose the kind you will use before you make a jig or buy one to be sure of compatibility.

The one tool you need is a jig to space the holes evenly. There are many commercially available jigs, but a shop-built jig can work just fine. I prefer jigs that use a router rather than a hand drill. They generally cut cleaner holes, but with a little extra care hand-drill-based jigs are fine. They are also easier to make and cheaper to buy. The disadvantage of shopmade jigs is that they wear and get sloppy after a few uses, but for the occasional bookcase this is fine.

Shop-built jigs are quick to make but lack the versatility of some commercial jigs and wear quickly.

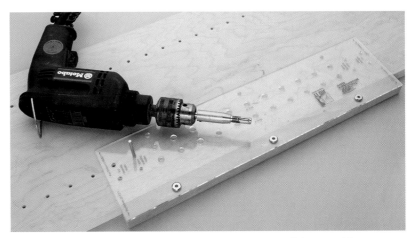

The Jig-It jig is inexpensive, easy to use, and good for quickly drilling a few holes. But it lacks the versatility and repeatability of more complex jigs.

The Veritas line-boring jig is complex, versatile, and good for repeatedly drilling the same series of holes in multiple case sides such as kitchen cabinets.

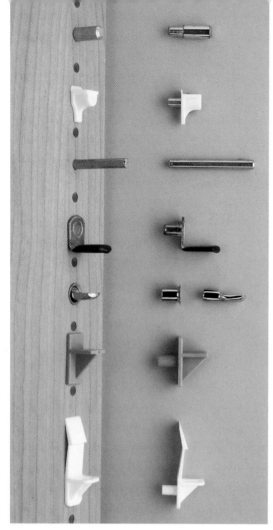

The cap nut combination (top) threads together and is perfect to use when you have access to both sides; the joint connector bolt (middle) uses threaded inserts, and the Confirmat Euro screw (bottom) has very deep threads, making it possible to take the screw out many times without losing holding strength.

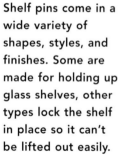

Shelf pins come in a wide variety of shapes, styles, and finishes. Some are made for holding up glass shelves, other types lock the shelf in place so it can't be lifted out easily.

I have bought and discarded several commercial jigs over the years, and they all have pluses and minuses. I now own three: two are pictured on p. 15, and the third, my favorite, I use for the Simple Tall Bookcase beginning on p. 32. All have different applications.

The Festo router-type jig used for the Simple Tall Bookcase is the main one I use for almost all my line-boring. Of the other two, the Veritas jig used to be my mainstay, but now I use it for those times when I have to drill holes in a piece that's already built. I use the small plastic Jig-It when I want to drill just a few holes very quickly.

Line-boring is easy. If you are careful with your layout, the process goes fast. Once the holes are drilled (standard hole-diameter choices are ¼ in. and 5mm) you need only insert the grommets and/or the shelf pins of your choice. What could be easier?

Knockdown fasteners Building a true knockdown bookcase is a whole science unto

itself, and I was disappointed not to include one in the book (a long story). The bookcase on pp. 162-181 does, however, separate into two parts and relies on one of the cooler knockdown fasteners on the market to accomplish this. Knockdown fasteners such as these as well as the connector bolts and Euro screws pictured above can be invaluable in a two-part bookcase where you need to attach the case to a base or two sections of case to one another.

Screws and nails Though I'm probably risking ridicule to say this, I routinely use screws to attach some parts of my furniture. Now, I don't use them everywhere, but I'm not above using a screw in some out-of-the-way spot to speed up construction. For example, connecting separate bases and backs is a good application. Do not, however, use drywall screws. Use screws specifically designed for furniture making. Drywall screws are thinner and not hardened sufficiently. The heads strip out easily, and they have a nasty habit of breaking off from the torque of twisting them in, usually when the project is just about done. "Cabinet screws," available through most woodworking supply catalogs, are much stronger and never break off when driving—so far in my experience.

Nails were often used to assist simple joinery in older pieces. A homeowner would possibly also have been the builder of a bookcase. Perfect joinery might not have been something he either had the tools or the expertise to produce. Add to this the state of glue technology in the past, and you can see why someone would throw in a nail or two. I have seen quite lovely country bookcases with dadoed shelves, as in the bookcase on pp. 68-79, aided by cut nails either driven into the end of a shelf or toenailed in from the underside.

PUTTING IT ALL TOGETHER

There is more to building a piece of furniture than making sure it is strong enough to support a load of books or fits the corner of the room you had in mind. So far we've broken the whole process into tiny bits and discussed each part, but one thing we haven't discussed is design—or, more important, good design.

There are many advantages to working from successful previous designs, either copying something you like or working from plans (like this book). This kind of path can help you build a design vocabulary, if you will, allowing you to mix and match ideas in your head or on paper or, for that matter, by actually building something. There is nothing quite as effective as standing in front of something you are building and figuring out why it doesn't look right—or better, why it does.

The following projects cover a lot of design ground. Some are based on designs from the past, some around a specific use, and some just came out of the mind of the builder. But no matter their source of inspiration, they are all good designs. This doesn't mean that you will like the look of every one, but they all meet their purpose (being bookcases) without having that be the only thing they have to say.

There is no better teacher than experience, and by building the projects in this book you'll get a guiding hand as you gain that experience and not encounter as many pitfalls as you would if you were just going it alone.

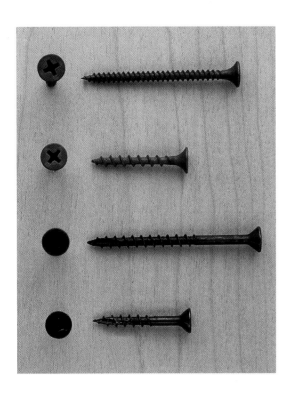
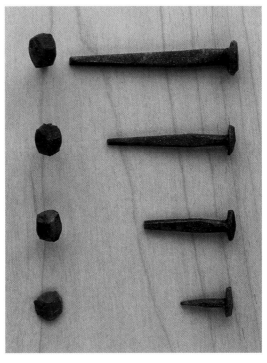

Far left: Drywall screws are on the top and sinker-style cabinet screws on the bottom. They look similar, but the cabinet screws are much stronger and can be driven by either a Phillips-head or a square-head driver.

Left: Reproduction cut nails are simple to use and offer a pleasing country look to any piece.

Simple
Short Bookcase

My three-year-old son loves two things: trains and books. It follows that he especially loves books about trains. What more perfect gift for him than a bookcase to hold his growing collection of books, trains, and especially his books on trains?

Looking around our house for a location to put it, I realized that the bookcase had to be less than 3 ft. wide to fit a wall in his room. Also, it could be no more than 4 ft. high or I'd have to build a stool so my son could reach the top shelf. And like most things I build for my home, it had to be really easy and fast. So I came up with this project, the Simple Short Bookcase.

This is an instructional bookcase, which means that I chose its attributes in part to clearly illustrate basic techniques. It's built of solid butternut, uses traditional joinery, and has fixed shelves. The sides have a gentle taper from 9 in. at the bottom to 7⅛ in. at the top. The sides also extend past the top shelf, making it a little more interesting and actually a little easier to build. A small (2-in.) radius at the top front edge of each side completes the package.

The case is quite easy to build, and only took a couple of days, including finishing. By the end of a weekend, my son was proudly taking his train books off the shelves (and when reminded, putting them back).

Simple Short Bookcase

This very simple bookcase is joined together with rabbets, dadoes, and glue. It has fixed shelves and a plywood back. The use of solid butternut, the tapered edges, and the radius top on the sides add considerably to what would otherwise be a plain piece.

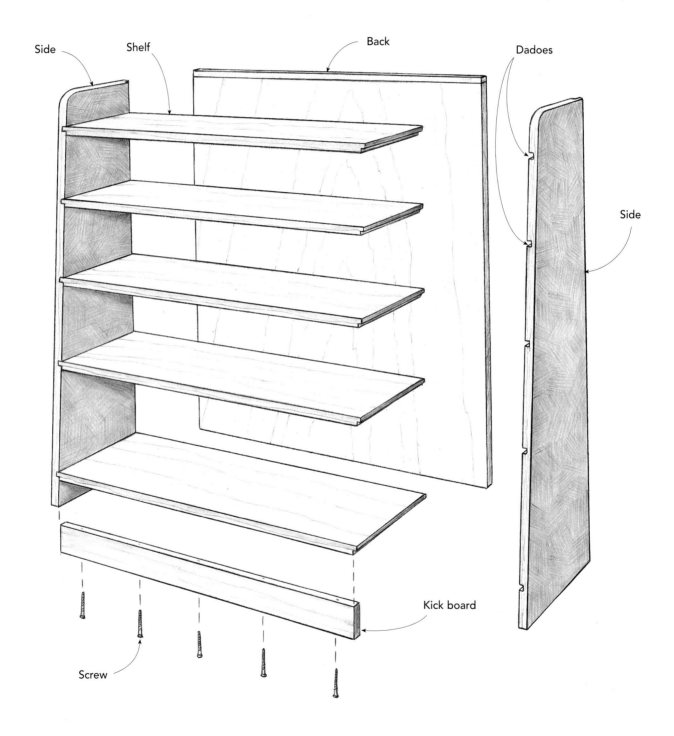

Side

Shelf

Back

Dadoes

Side

Kick board

Screw

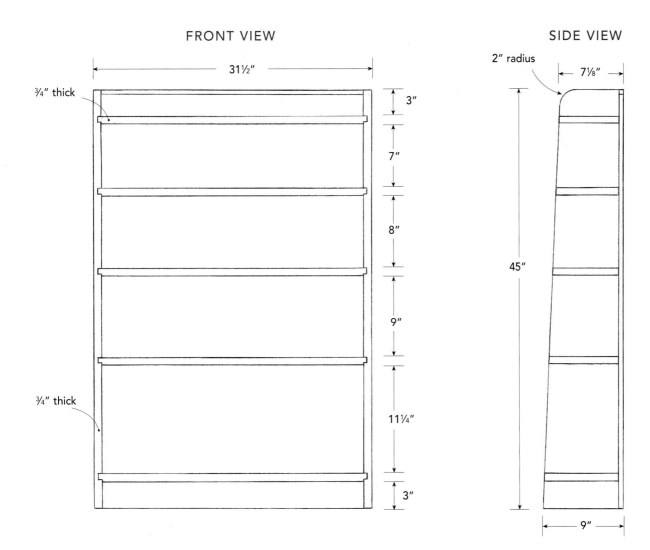

FRONT VIEW

31½"

¾" thick

3"

7"

8"

9"

11¼"

¾" thick

3"

SIDE VIEW

2" radius

7⅛"

45"

9"

CUT LIST FOR SIMPLE SHORT BOOKCASE

Carcase and Shelves

2	Sides	45 in. x 9 in. x ¾ in.
5	Shelves	30¾ in. x 9 in. x ¾ in.
1	Edging for top of back	30¾ in. x ½ in. x ¾ in.
1	Kick board	30 in. x 3 in. x ¾ in.
1	Back	30¾ in. x 44¼ in. x ½ in.

Hardware

5	Screws	3 in. x #8

All parts are solid butternut except the back, which is ½-in. maple plywood.

BUILDING THE BOOKCASE STEP-BY-STEP

THE JOINERY in this bookcase is a little fussy, but the scale is such that all the parts are easy to manage. This allows me to do almost all the work on the table saw, which is by far the quickest way to cut this joinery. In fact, once the table saw is set up, the joinery goes very quickly, and you're on to the more fun aspects of furniture making—shaping and styling. Some simple jigsaw, router, and sanding work completes the bookcase.

PREPARING STOCK

A cut list and drawing

1. Make a drawing of the bookcase to give you a look at scale and proportion and to allow you to work out construction details.
2. Write up a cut list with rough dimensions and final dimensions (from the cut list on p. 21). A good rule of thumb to figure rough dimensions is to add 1 in. to the width, 3 in. to the length, and 25 percent to the thickness for rough solid stock. Vary these additions depending on the condition of the stock. Don't apply the rule to sheet goods like plywood.
3. Pick out your stock using the rough dimension list. It will help keep the parts straight, and ensure that you have enough to work with when you shape the parts.

Milling to thickness

1. Flatten and thickness all the stock at one time since the bookcase is small and there are only nine solid wood pieces.
2. Size the parts to the rough dimensions cut list. You can work faster at this stage by milling to the numbers (see **photo A**).
3. Rip the parts to finished width and crosscut them to length.

Photo A: Rough-dimension cut lists help you keep track of the parts before they are recognizable as you mill them to size.

CUTTING THE JOINERY

Laying out the joints

Because the sides continue past the top shelf, you can use the same joint, a shallow dado, to connect all the shelves.

1. Butt and clamp the sides together with their ends flush.

2. Mark the location of each dado across both sides on their inside faces. This ensures that the shelf spacing will be exactly the same.

3. Mark the bottom and back of each side so you don't mix them up later.

4. Mark the location of the tenons on the shelves and clearly mark the top face of each shelf (see "Layout of Dadoes and Stub Tenons").

SHELF JOINTS, SIDE, AND BACK

The only two joints used to assemble this bookcase are dadoes and rabbets.

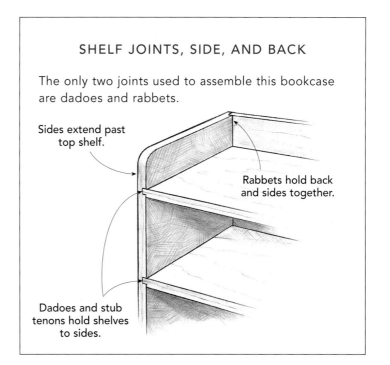

Sides extend past top shelf.

Rabbets hold back and sides together.

Dadoes and stub tenons hold shelves to sides.

LAYOUT OF DADOES AND STUB TENONS

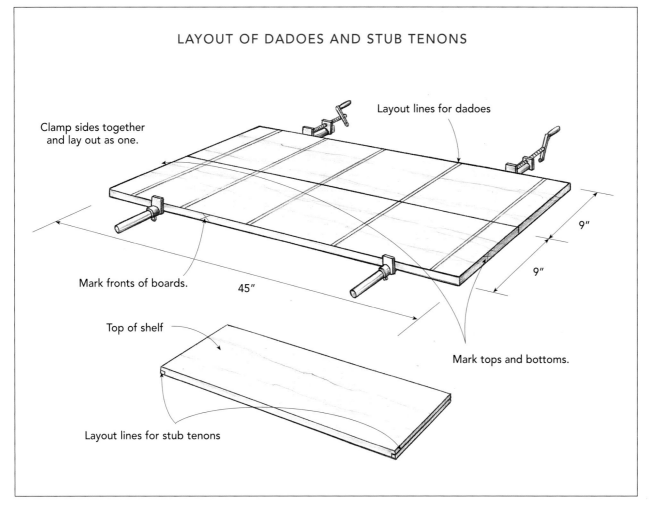

Clamp sides together and lay out as one.

Layout lines for dadoes

Mark fronts of boards.

45″

9″

9″

Top of shelf

Layout lines for stub tenons

Mark tops and bottoms.

Photo B: **A short stop block positioned at the back of the fence helps keep the dadoes consistent and reduces the risk of binding the board in the cut.**

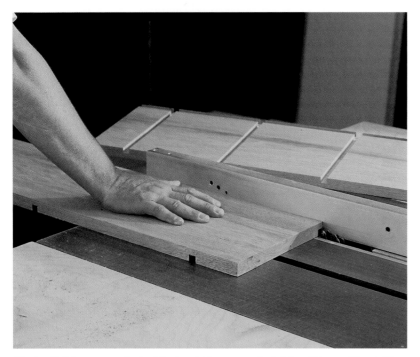

Photo C: **The same dado blade at the same height setting will cut the rabbets for the back.**

Cutting the dadoes in the sides and the rabbets on the shelves

You can use the table saw to cut all the joints because the sides and shelves are so small. On a larger bookcase, you would have to bring the tool to the wood and use a router or a plow plane to cut the joints.

1. Clamp a stop block to the back of the saw fence to register against the end of each side. The stop block keeps the workpiece from binding between the blade and the fence.
2. Set the fence to cut one set of opposite dadoes in each side. Then reset the fence to cut another set of dadoes (see **photo B**).
3. Cut the dadoes with a ½-in.-wide dado head using the miter gauge to guide the sides. The exact depth is not critical, but should be consistent. Cut no deeper than half the thickness of the stock, or to ⅜ in.

4. Start cutting the dadoes from one end in toward the middle of the side. When you cut the middle shelf dado, turn the board around and work back the other way to avoid having too little stock resting on the miter gauge.

The stock must be straight and square for this method to work. If it's not, errors will accumulate, and misaligned shelves and a twisted bookcase will result.

5. Set your rip fence so it just clears the dado head and leave the dado head set at the same height.

6. Rip-cut the rabbets on the inside rear edge of the sides (see **photo C**). This joint will house the back. You may have a little whisper of wood on the edge of the joint. If it doesn't just fall off, hit with a sanding block.

Cutting the stub tenons on the shelf ends

Since the shelves aren't very long you can cut the stub tenons with the same dado head and a shopmade carrier that rides on your fence and holds the shelves on end. If you don't have a carrier like this or don't wish to make one, Delta sells a table-saw tenoning jig that works as well. The joint can also be cut with the workpiece horizontal on the table saw or with a router and rabbeting bit.

1. Test the carrier's setup with scrap pieces until you get it cutting the right thickness.

2. Test-fit the scrap pieces in the side dadoes. The fit of this joint is crucial to the strength of the piece as a whole. The tighter the joints, the stronger the case. You should have to apply some pressure to assemble a dry joint, but you shouldn't have to hammer it home.

3. When the dado head is set up properly, run the shelf ends over it, making sure that the same side of each shelf is facing the fence. Use a piece of scrap to back up the exit point of the dado head (see **photo D**).

Tip: Always back up the workpiece in a dado cut with a sacrificial scrap of wood to prevent tearout.

Photo D: A simple shopmade carrier will guide the shelf ends over the dado blade to tenon the ends.

Photo E: Draw the profile of the bookcase directly on the board in heavy pencil lines so you can clearly see where to cut.

Photo F: A jigsaw is the quickest and simplest way to cut the taper and the radius in one operation.

SHAPING THE PARTS

Laying out the profile of the sides

The profile of the sides is composed of two simple shapes: a gentle taper from the bottom up and a 2-in. radius at the top.

1. Draw the taper with a straightedge from top to bottom.
2. Scribe the radius at the top with a compass. To find the center of the radius, spin the dividers from two points, one that is 2 in. down the taper from the edge, and the other that is 2 in. in from the taper line. The intersection of these arcs is the center of the radius (see **photo E**).
3. Cut to within ⅛ in. of the line with a jigsaw (see **photo F**).
4. Put a smooth edge on the sides, using a board with a straightedge as a guide and a router fitted with a top-bearing straight bit, also called a pattern bit (see **photo G**).
5. Smooth the radius portions by hand with a sanding block.

Ripping angles on the front edge of the shelves to match the sides

The taper of the sides requires that the front edges of the shelves be ripped at the same angle, in this case at about 2 degrees.

1. To determine the angle, you can measure it off the drawing using a protractor or, to be extra certain, off the sides.
2. Rip the angle first on all the shelves, making sure the same side of each shelf is up (see **photo H**).
3. Fit the shelves in their grooves with the front edges flush with the sides, and then mark the back edges at the rabbet to get their respective depths.
4. Rip the shelf backs to width, remembering to readjust the sawblade to 90 degrees.

Photo G: With a straight plywood board to guide the router, trim the edge of the case side with a straight bit. Don't worry about smoothing the radius this way. It's best done by hand later.

Photo H: Rip the small angle on the front edge of the shelves on the table saw.

Tip: Wait until you have the rest of the bookcase dry-fit together to cut the back to size. This way, you can measure the real dimensions you need.

Cutting the back to size

The plywood back should run the full height of the bookcase. It fits into the rabbets in the sides and butts up against the back edges of the shelves.

1. To cover the top edge of the plywood, attach a ½-in. by ¾-in. strip of butternut with #10 biscuits and glue (see **photo I**). The biscuits help align the strip and keep it in place during clamping.
2. Cut the back to size.

ASSEMBLY

Pre-assembly

1. Sand all the parts that will be difficult to reach after the bookcase is assembled. These include the shelves and the inside faces of the sides and back.
2. Be careful not to sand the ends of the shelves that fit into the grooves unless you need to adjust the thickness to fit better.
3. Dry-fit the whole bookcase. This is your chance to make any minor corrections in joint fit and alignment. It's also a chance to make

Photo I: Use biscuits to align the solid butternut strip on the top of the back.

Tip: It's a really good idea to sand everything smooth before assembly because it's far easier to sand parts that are flat than to sand into and around corners.

DRY-RUN ASSEMBLIES

Yellow glue sets very quickly—in a matter of minutes. This makes it good to know how long a glue-up will take, especially if it could be longer than the open time of the glue.

To make sure, I often do a complete dry-run assembly. I apply all the clamps that will be necessary during actual glue-up to make sure all the joints close up tight and so I can position clamps where they're needed. I also normally mark the mating tenons and dadoes. If they get mixed up during glue-up, it's a mess to pull things apart and get them in the right places.

I sometimes go so far as pretending to apply glue. This may sound funny for a professional woodworker, like a politician practicing how to lie; but if there is a lot of glue area, knowing how much time it will take to spread the glue can be a big help. If it is too long, you'll need to break your glue-ups into two parts. This bookcase is so small that glue-up time isn't an important issue, but in the larger projects it will be.

Photo J: An acid brush is small enough to spread glue evenly in the dadoes of the sides.

sure you have everything you need for glue-up and can work quickly and smoothly within the open time of the glue (see "Dry-Run Assemblies").

Final glue-up

1. Gather all the clamps, glue, rags, and other tools and supplies you will need. You don't want to be looking for something during glue-up.

2. Lay out both sides with dadoes and rabbets up and back to back.

3. Spread glue into the joints with a small acid brush (see **photo J**). Don't just squeeze a bead of glue from the bottle into the dadoes. You won't get a good indication of how much glue you're using. Don't put any glue on the tenon or on the shoulder; it doesn't add any strength and ends up just making a mess.

4. Work from one side, inserting tenons in dadoes, one at a time, and aligning the back edges with the rabbet for the back before pushing them home. In a well-fitting joint it may be impossible to slide the shelves sideways once fully inserted.

5. Use a dead-blow hammer for extra persuasion when necessary. A hammer and a block of wood are just as good—except that you need an extra hand to hold the block.

6. Lay the second side on top of the open shelf tenons (see **photo K**). By this time, any glue brushed into these grooves has had a chance to set just enough so it won't run when you place this side.

Photo K: Glue-up can be a hectic time, so make sure you have all the clamps and pieces ready to go and proceed in a quick but orderly fashion.

7. Draw the joints tight with clamps. On a case this small, two clamps per shelf should be all you need. Sometimes a caul may be necessary to put pressure on the center of the joint.

8. Check the case for square by measuring the diagonals once everything is well clamped and the joints are tight.

9. If the case is out in any direction (i.e., shaped like a parallelogram), apply a clamp over the longer diagonal until the glue dries (see **photo L**). Minor out-of-square issues can usually be taken care of when the back is installed, provided the back is square and fits just right.

10. If you have a lot of glue squeeze-out, try to scrape most of it off when it's a little rubbery. A clean, damp cloth should take care of the remainder.

11. Remove any remaining glue squeeze-out with a sharp chisel when dry.

12. Sand any spots you smeared with glue during cleanup, or the glue will hamper the penetration of the finish.

Attaching the back and the kick board

1. When the glue is dry, unclamp the carcase and attach the last two pieces: the back and the kick board.

2. Screw the back to the rabbets and to the backs of the shelves with 1-in. trim-head screws. Trim-head screws are thin screws with a very small head, about 3/16 in. in diameter. I use these to attach the back because the rabbet is only 3/8 in. wide, and larger-head screws are just too big.

3. Butt-fit the base piece, or kick board, tight between the sides and screw it in place through countersunk holes into the bottom shelf (see "Attaching the Kick Board").

Tip: *Breaking the
edges is important
because otherwise
you risk having the
edges splinter.*

ATTACHING THE KICK BOARD

The kick board is simply screwed through countersunk holes into the underside of the bottom shelf.

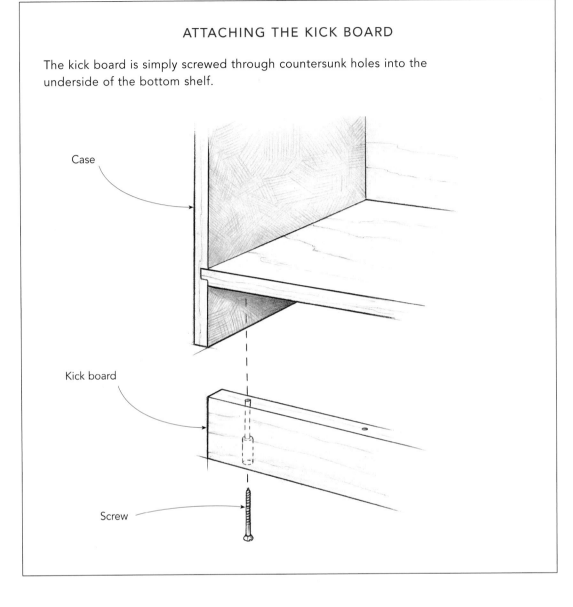

Case

Kick board

Screw

FINISHING UP

Final sanding and finish application

1. When the glue is dry, sand the outside of the bookcase to 180 grit.

2. Break all the edges by lightly sanding them with 180 grit. It may seem as if you'll lose some definition, but that's only a risk if you go overboard.

3. Remove the back to make finishing easier.

4. Apply the finish. I recommend a simple wax finish for this project. It's a very under-rated and underused finish. It looks and feels wonderful, and for applications like a bookcase, it's more than adequate protection. A wax finish takes a lot of elbow work, but it's almost impossible to do wrong—if you apply too much, it can be hard to rub out to a good shine, but that's about the worst that can happen. I used butcher's wax. It adds only a small amount of color, is easy to find, and is self-stripping. This means it dissolves itself when a new coat of wax is reapplied, so it doesn't build up and dull the finish you are trying to shine.

SIMPLE TALL BOOKCASE

My wife and I have a room we call our office. It isn't really "ours" but hers. I do my writing in my shop. The dust is a little rough on the computer, but it's my space. Anyway, "our" office used to be what we called the junk room. You know, every house has one. It's the place where everything that doesn't have a place ends up, generally in piles on the floor.

The junk-room conversion, however, was never really completed to "our" office because there was still a certain amount of stuff, mostly magazines, piled here and there. As the magazines were all mine, it was my job to get them up off the floor. So, I designed and built a tall, simple bookcase, which I gave the catchy name of Simple Tall Bookcase, to get all the magazines off the floor.

This bookcase is similar to the one on pp. 18-31 in that it's very basic in design but different in a number of important ways. First of all, it's made from edge-banded plywood, not solid wood. I used biscuit joinery to put it together and added adjustable shelves above and below a fixed central shelf. I sized it to fit a sliver of wall between two doors and to hold my entire collection of back issues of *Fine Woodworking*, *Fine Homebuilding*, and *Home Furniture* with room left over. It's simple to build, and it holds a relatively large amount of stuff. It also doesn't look too bad.

Simple Tall Bookcase

THIS BOOKCASE HAS a very simple boxlike shape with shelves, top, and bottom, all looking essentially identical. The interest is in the details, which include the five adjustable shelves in between the top and bottom fixed shelves, and a center fixed shelf for support. The construction is very simple, using only biscuits, even on the kick board.

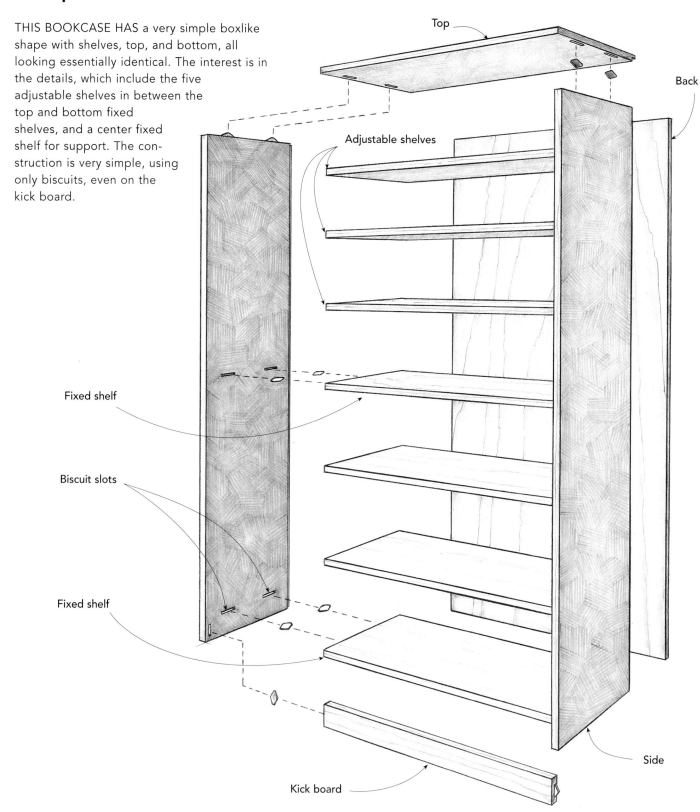

Top

Back

Adjustable shelves

Fixed shelf

Biscuit slots

Fixed shelf

Side

Kick board

FRONT VIEW

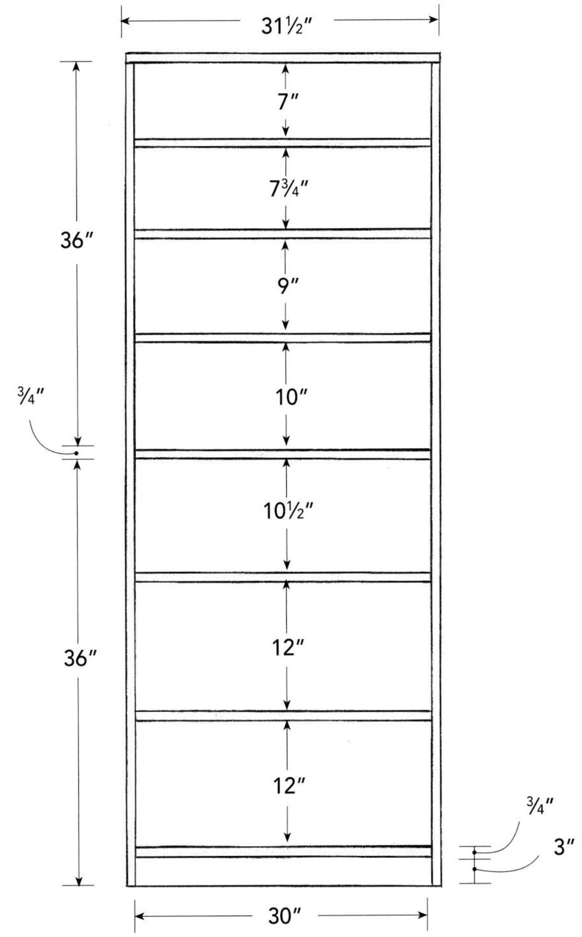
31½″
7″
7¾″
9″
10″
10½″
12″
12″
36″
¾″
36″
¾″
3″
30″

SIDE VIEW

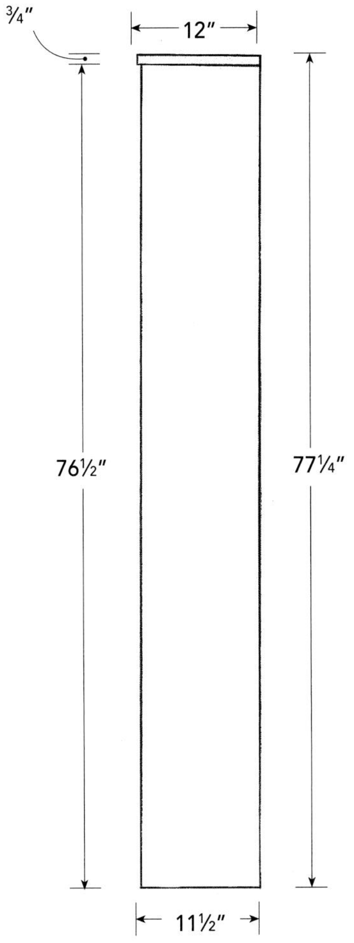
¾″
12″
76½″
77¼″
11½″

SHELF CONNECTIONS

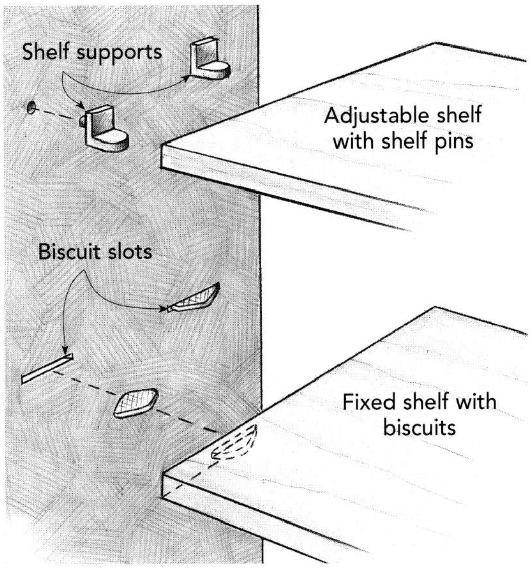
Shelf supports
Adjustable shelf with shelf pins
Biscuit slots
Fixed shelf with biscuits

CUT LIST FOR SIMPLE TALL BOOKCASE

Carcase and Shelves		
2	Sides	76½ in. x 11½ in. x ¾ in.
1	Back	76⅞ in. x 30¾ in. x ½ in.
7	Shelves	30 in. x 10⅞ in. x ¾ in.
1	Top	31½ in. x 12 in. x ¾ in.
1	Kick board	30 in. x 3 in. x ¾ in.
	Edge-banding	35 ft. x ⅞ in.
Hardware		
20	Shelf pins	

All parts are ¾-in. maple plywood except the back, which is ½-in. maple plywood.

BUILDING THE BOOKCASE STEP-BY-STEP

BOOKCASES OF THIS type are the workaday bookcases we all need in our lives to organize our stuff. They won't win any design contests, but I rather like their honesty. What will set this bookcase apart from the unpainted-furniture-store variety is attention to detail. Treat these simple cases the same way you do all your furniture, keeping the fit and finish as crisp as you can. This is a piece with strong edges. It's all veneer and edge tape. There's nowhere to soften it, so it has to be just so. Just because it's simple doesn't mean it should be built with any less care. People will notice!

LAYING OUT THE PLYWOOD PARTS

The size of this bookcase, 31½ in. wide by 77¼ in. high by 11½ in. deep, takes into account the size of a sheet of plywood and its design limitations (see "Designing with

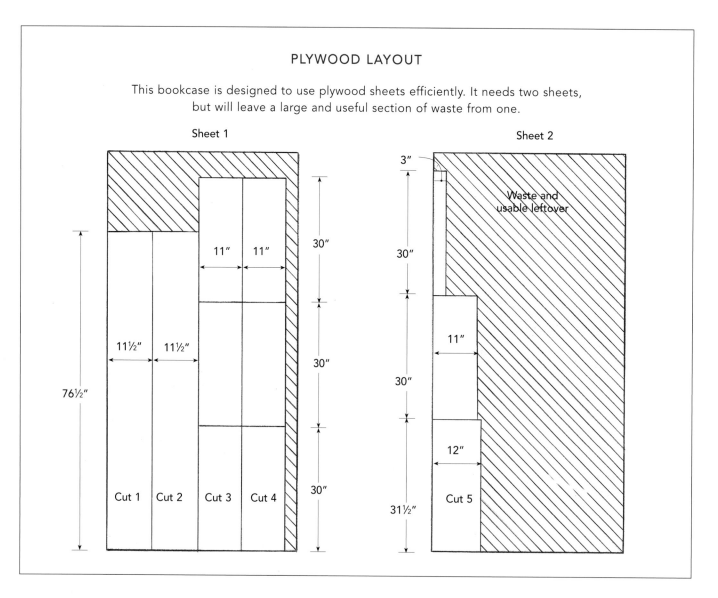

PLYWOOD LAYOUT

This bookcase is designed to use plywood sheets efficiently. It needs two sheets, but will leave a large and useful section of waste from one.

Plywood"). The 11½-in. depth of the piece is sized to be cut efficiently from two sheets of ¾-in. plywood. My magazines also happen to fit it quite nicely. And it has no vertical span longer than 3 ft., beyond which the plywood might bow.

1. Prepare a drawing and cut list, and then lay out the parts on the sheets of plywood (see "Plywood Layout").

2. Always add ⅛ in. to the thickness of your lines to compensate for the thickness of the sawblade. Also don't measure in exactly from any of the edges. Add ⅛ in. or more so that you can later trim the factory edge, which is usually a little uneven or beat-up in some way.

MAKING THE PARTS AND CUTTING THE JOINERY

Cutting parts to size

Rip and crosscut the plywood parts to finished sizes. For information on how the application of edge tape will affect overall dimensions, see "Designing with Edge Tape" on p. 38.

Rabbeting for the back

1. Cut the rabbets for the plywood back along the inside edge of the sides and rear edge of the top. Use a router fitted with a ½-in. bearing-guided rabbeting bit (see **photo A**).

2. For the sides, run the rabbet all the way from end to end.

3. For the top, stop the rabbet short of both ends about ⅜ in. This dimension is not critical—judge it by eye. Just be careful not to rout through to the edges since they show.

4. Don't square up the rounded end in the rabbet with a chisel just yet. Wait until after the case is assembled (but before you fit the back).

DESIGNING WITH PLYWOOD

Plywood has many advantages. You don't need to mill it to thickness, it generally doesn't have serious warps or twists, and it's strong in every direction, unlike solid wood.

Its limitations, though, are often overlooked. One, it comes in sheets no longer than 96 in. If you want a 97-in.-tall bookcase made of plywood, you're out of luck. Its width poses the same problem. Making plywood bookcases demands that you design with 96 in. by 48 in. in mind at all times. To get the most out of a sheet, you don't want to design a bookcase with 25-in.-wide by 96-in.-tall sides because you will only be able to get one side out of a sheet and have 23 in. of waste.

Photo A: Cutting the rabbet in the sides is easy with a router and a ½-in. piloted bit. It's especially useful for the stopped cut on the top edge.

Tip: The veneer
surface on plywood
is thin and easily
damaged. The less
it's slid across tables
and otherwise
moved, the better.
There is nothing
worse than discov-
ering a scratch
that's too deep to
sand out.

Laying out and cutting the biscuit slots

There are 28 biscuit slots in this bookcase. They are not all the same type of slot and fall roughly into three categories: slots on the edges of a board, slots at right angles to an edge, and slots in the middle of a board's face (see "Three Basic Biscuit Joints" on p. 40).

1. Work out the location of the fixed shelf if you need shelves spaced differently than shown. An inch or so in one direction won't really compromise the structure, but don't go more than a few inches either way.

2. Lay out and cut the biscuit slots according to the rough locations in "Biscuit Slot Layout." Mark the slots with a simple line centered where you want the biscuit. Leave

DESIGNING WITH EDGE TAPE

Applying edge tape to the parts will add some thickness, but I don't compensate for it when I rip parts to size. There is a method to my madness.

First, edge tape is usually less than $1/16$ in. thick, which is an almost meaningless increment in a bookcase of this kind.

Second, most of the parts will have this $1/16$ in. added in the same plane. For example, both the sides and shelves will have tape applied to their front edges, so their relationship doesn't change.

Third, there are two places where the added edge tape stands proud, and in both cases it is to the advantage of the design. The top will become $1/8$ in. wider than the case ($1/16$ in. on each side), giving a little definition to the otherwise featureless sides. Also the kick board ends up recessed an extra $1/8$ in. To get this effect, however, you have to remember to cut the biscuit slots before you edge-tape.

These are minor details, but thinking through the whole design before you lay out the parts is a good habit to get into. Well practiced, you can clear up confusing details, find solutions, and prevent mistakes.

Biscuit Slot Layout

The entire bookcase is held together with biscuit joints. All centerline measurements for biscuit layout are made from the back of the shelves and from the edge of the rabbet on the sides and top. This is because the shelves are set back $1/8$ in. from the front of the case.

UNDERSIDE OF TOP

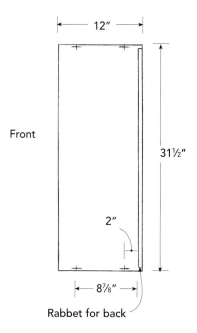

12"

Front

31½"

2"

8⅞"

Rabbet for back

End   2"

KICK BOARD
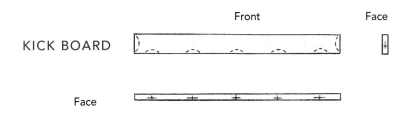
Front
Face

Face

CENTER FIXED SHELF

Front

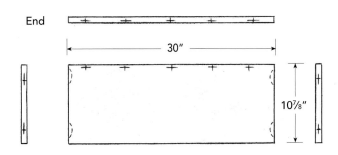

UNDERSIDE OF BOTTOM FIXED SHELF

End

30″

10⅞″

30″

10⅞″

8⅞″

INSIDE OF RIGHT SIDE

Front

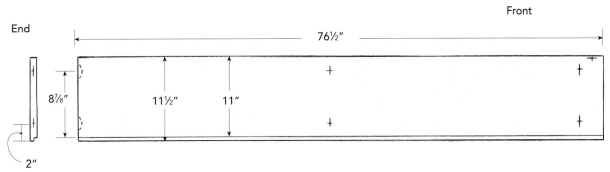

End

76½″

8⅞″   11½″   11″

2″

INSIDE OF LEFT SIDE

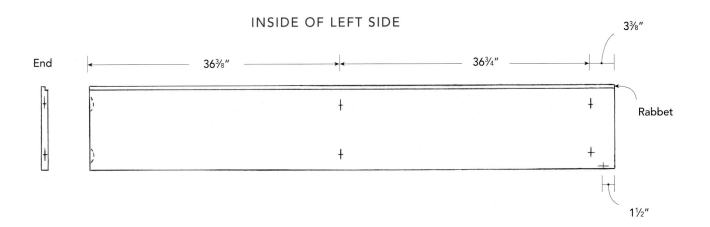

End

36⅜″   36¾″   3⅜″

Rabbet

1½″

Photo B: Cut biscuit slots in the ends of the fixed shelves and at the top of the sides.

enough room on each side of every slot for other biscuits or the edge of the board.

3. Cut the slots in the ends of the fixed shelves, at the top of the sides, and in the kick board (see **photo B**). These are cuts in the edge of a board. Most of the biscuit slots in this project are of this type.

4. Cut the slots in the top piece. These are the only slots you cut in a board's face at the edge (see **photo C**).

5. Cut the slots for the center fixed shelf and base. These slots are in the face of the sides but not near an edge. You must make a temporary fence or stop to register against the base of the joiner. Instead of searching the shop for an appropriate piece of scrap, just use the mating shelf for a stop (see **photo D**).

THREE BASIC BISCUIT JOINTS

Biscuit joinery has revolutionized woodworking in the last 30 years. Biscuit joints are easy to cut, can be very accurate, and are super strong. They have every advantage, and few limitations. There are, however, a few tricks to learn for cutting them. On this bookcase, they fall into roughly three categories.

Slots on the edges of a board

This is certainly the easiest type of biscuit slot to cut, and the one you see used most. With the fence set at 90 degrees and lying flat on the face of the board, plunge into the edge. The machine is no problem to hold, and the plunge is easy to control.

Slots at right angles to an edge

This type of biscuit slot is similar to the first type, but the orientation is reversed. The fence registers against the edge as the joiner cuts into the face. It's the most difficult type of slot to cut because the fence doesn't have much to register against. Make sure the face of the joiner lies flat on the workpiece, and hold it there as steadily as you can in the cut.

An option is to clamp a square block to the opposite side of the board flush with the edge of the workpiece. This will give the joiner more stability. But be careful: If the block is slightly off or out of square, your slot will be as well.

Slots in the middle of a board's face

These types of slots are easily cut, and the fence set at 90 degrees flat on the workpiece is very stable. You must make a temporary fence or stop block, though, to register against the base of the joiner.

The difficulty in cutting these slots is laying them out and keeping track of the direction to cut. You have to be able to measure from the joiner's base to the centerline of the cutter, and then translate that measurement into a location for the stop block so the shelf and the side slots line up just right. Take your time and think about where the shelf and slots should be before marking or cutting anything: There's a bit of Zen involved with biscuit joinery.

6. Cut the slots in the sides for the kick board. As the kick board is set back from the front of the bottom shelf ⅛ in., cut the slots in the underside of the shelf using the ¾-in. setting on the biscuit joiner and cut the slots in the mating edge of the kick board using the ½-in. setting.

7. Cut the slots in the ends of the kick board in the same way as in step 6. Remember the slots in the side have to be set in an extra ⅛ in. for everything to line up.

8. Dry-fit the piece to make sure it goes together properly. Common problems include misalignment of biscuit slots and slots that are cut too shallow.

Laying out and drilling the shelf-pin holes

To cut the shelf-pin holes, I use a Festo jig (see Sources on pp. 182-183) and router fitted with a 5mm bit (see **photo E** on p. 42). You can also use a number of other good commercial jigs described on pp. 14-16, or make your own.

1. Locate the jig a specific distance from the front and back edges as well as top to bottom. As a general rule drill holes 2 in. in from the front and back edges of a 12-in.-wide case side (that's one-sixth the total width as a rule of thumb), and leave 6 in. to 8 in. at top and bottom without holes.

Tip: To ensure that the shelves are horizontal (important in my book), be consistent in how you register the layout lines. What you do on one side, do on the other. Otherwise the errors will accumulate.

Photo C: The biscuit slots in the top are cut on the edge but at a right angle. This is a difficult kind of cut to keep stable, so go slowly and carefully.

Photo D: Use a shelf as a stop block, aligned on the edge of where the shelf intersects the side, to support the biscuit joiner when cutting the slots in the sides.

Photo E: The Festo boring jig makes routing accurate holes in the sides quick and easy.

Photo F: With an edge-banding iron, I apply banding to all edges that show.

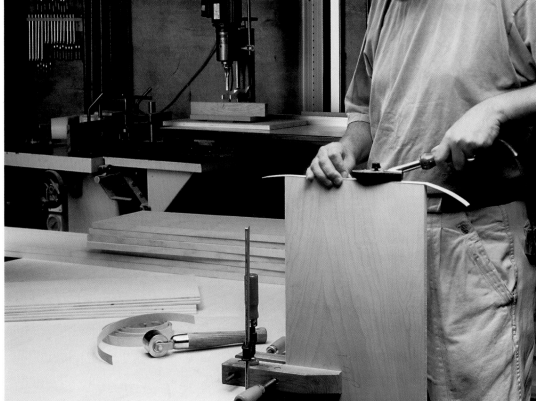

Tip: To fix mis-aligned slots that won't show, simply glue a biscuit into the slot, trim it flush, and then recut the slots when the glue dries.

Photo G: Assemble the bottom shelf and kick board before you glue up the entire case. This will make the over-all glue-up less complicated.

2. Drill the shelf-pin holes in the sides. The important thing is to consistently drill two rows of evenly spaced holes on each side that line up with the rows on the opposing side.

Edge-banding shelves

Before assembly you'll want to band all the edges that show, including the front edge of all the shelves, the front edge of the sides, the front edge of the top, and the side edges of the top. I use iron-on veneer tape for this, which is available from many woodworking suppliers. I have an "edge-banding iron" for applying this tape, but a regular household clothing iron set on the dry or no-steam setting works just fine.

1. Break off a piece of tape a little longer than you need and, starting at one end, hold it on the edge and apply heat and pressure until the glue softens under the iron (see **photo F**).

2. Move along the edge a few inches at a time with the iron until the tape is stuck.

3. Trim off the extra length of edge-banding by scoring it lightly on the underside and breaking it off.

4. As the edge tape is slightly wider than ³⁄₄ in., sand it with an orbital sander to make it flush to the shelf faces. Then sand the ends flush with a sanding block.

ASSEMBLY AND FINISHING

Preparing for glue-up

1. Sand all the parts up through 150 grit. I find this to be more than adequate surface preparation before spraying the bookcase with water-based lacquer (though there is some debate over how fine a grit one should sand to under a sprayed finish).

2. Double-check that you have everything you need (clamps, etc.) before you put glue into anything.

Photo H: Check for square and reposition clamps if necessary to adjust. Double or triple up clamps if you don't have any long enough to put pressure on the top.

Tip: If you don't have clamps long enough to reach the full length of the bookcase, you can double and even triple them up. It gets tricky, but it works.

Attaching the kick board to the bottom shelf

1. Glue up the kick board and bottom shelf before you glue up the case (see **photo G** on p. 43). This cuts down the time and the amount of clamps needed during glue-up.
2. Make sure the ends of the kick board and the shelf are perfectly flush during this glue-up because there is no way to fix this after the fact. If you sand them flush, they will not be as wide as the shelves.

Gluing and clamping the case

1. Glue biscuits into all the face slots on both sides.
2. Lay one side down with the biscuits facing up.

3. Glue and position the bottom shelf/kick board on its mating biscuits, then move to the center fixed shelf, and glue and position it.
4. Attach the other side on top of this assembly and clamp across the case, front and back, at both shelf locations.
5. Check the case for square and adjust clamps, if necessary. Check for square now rather than when the case is fully clamped because the clamp pressure along sides this long will often distort or bow them. Any minor out-of-square problems in the case will usually be corrected when you fit the back.
6. Clamp the top, front and back, on both sides (see **photo H**). Check for square again.

Installing the back

The last part of the assembly stage is to make and fit the back.

1. When the case glue is dry, remove the clamps, clean up any glue squeeze-out with a sharp chisel, and do any touch-up sanding necessary.
2. Lay the case on its face and square up the top corners of the rabbet with a sharp chisel (these were left from the routing earlier).
3. Measure the opening created by the rabbets and cut some ½-in. plywood to fit snugly.
4. Sand the back to 150 grit.
5. Mark out and drill pilot holes around the perimeter and across the backs of the shelves for 1-in. trim-head screws (see **photo I**).
6. Screw the back in place.

Applying the finish

I finished this piece with a clear water-based finish called Resisthane, which is manufactured by Hydrocote (see Sources on pp. 182-183). I have been using water-based finishes for more than 10 years and am very happy with the results I get from this particular product. There isn't space to get into all the details of applying a spray finish, but if you're interested in trying it and need further guidance, I recommend *Spray Finishing* (The Taunton Press, 1998).

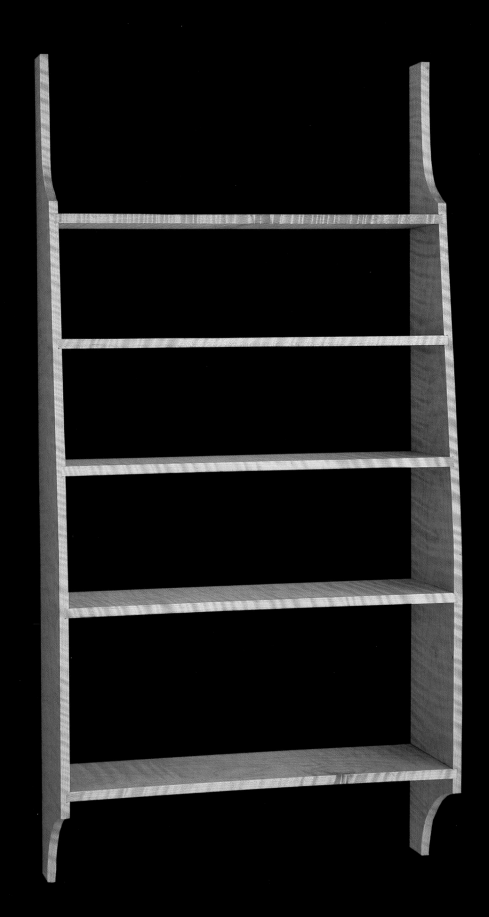

SHAKER-STYLE WALL SHELF

There is an intimacy to small wall shelves. Some woodworkers detail small shelves with ornamentation, turning them into little jewels that could almost be displayed on their own. Others are more subtle, relying on simple, but elegant, style and flawless execution.

This Shaker-style shelf was originally designed and built by Peter Turner, a woodworker in Portland, Maine. He has one in his kitchen as a spice shelf. In fact, he designed the size and shelf configuration around this application. But Turner gave his shelf a refined design to make it equally at home displaying some special objects.

I have a growing collection of miniature liquor bottles constantly in need of more display space. My plan was to take the best ones and place them on this shelf. Fate had other plans, however: The shelf was sent to be photographed for this book, and it's being used, ironically, as an elegant spice shelf in the photographer's kitchen.

Turner's inspiration to build this piece came from a drawing of a peg-hung Shaker shelf in Ejner Handberg's book, *Shop Drawings of Shaker Furniture and Woodenware* (Berkshire Traveler Press, 1975). The shelf sides in Handberg's drawing are curved on top but straight at the bottom. Peter added another curve at the bottom, experimenting with the curves until he found one he liked. Handberg's shelf also hung from a wall-mounted peg rail.

Shaker-Style Wall Shelf

THIS SMALL SHAKER-STYLE WALL SHELF in curly maple has only seven parts: five shelves and two sides. The shelves join the sides with sliding dovetails. The curves at the top and bottom are determined by eye.

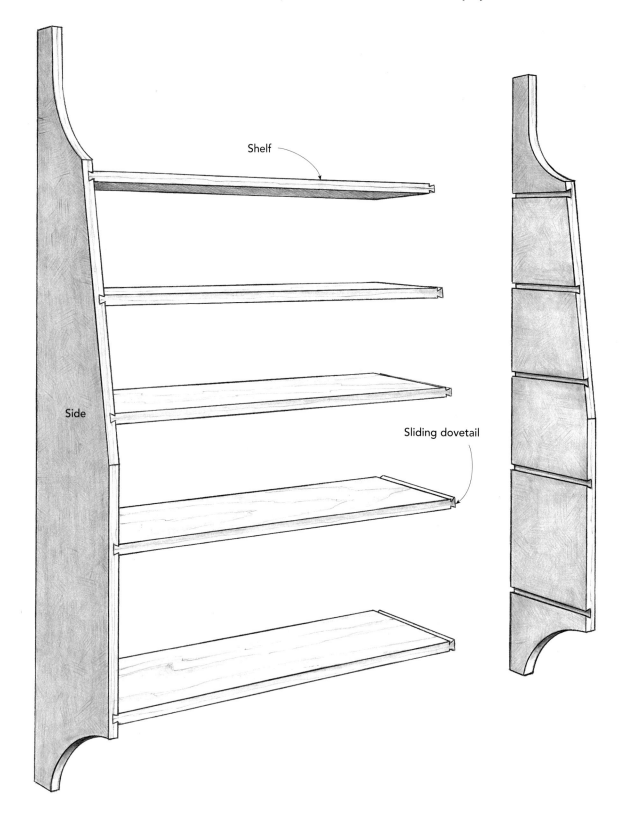

Shelf

Side

Sliding dovetail

ELEVATION   SIDE VIEW

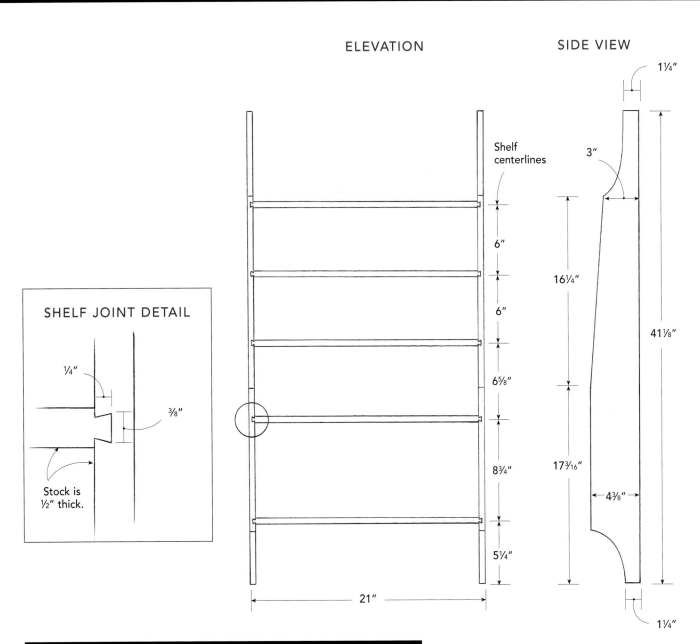

1¼"

Shelf
centerlines

3"

6"

16¼"

SHELF JOINT DETAIL

6"

41⅛"

¼"

6⅝"

⅜"

8¾"

17³⁄₁₆"

Stock is
½" thick.

4⅜"

5¼"

21"

1¼"

CUT LIST FOR SHAKER-STYLE WALL SHELF

Carcase and Shelves

2	Sides	41⅛ in. x 4⅜ in. x ½ in.
5	Shelves	20½ in. x 4⅜ in. x ½ in.

Hardware

Shelf hangers

All parts are solid curly maple.

BUILDING THE BOOKCASE STEP-BY-STEP

THIS IS A FAIRLY SIMPLE and quick project. The most difficult aspect (which really isn't) is cutting the sliding dovetails. The Shakers used dadoes, which are simpler, and you can certainly do the same. Dadoes aren't as strong, but in a project like this, it shouldn't matter. Routing the slots in the sides is relatively easy, but the long tails on the ends of each shelf take some patience. I use two router jigs for the process: one for the slots and one for the tails. And I use a plywood pattern and flush-trimming router bit for making identical curves and tapers on the sides.

PREPARING STOCK AND JOINERY

Thicknessing the curly maple parts

1. Mill all the parts at once to ½ in. thick to ensure consistency. For tips on how to work the curly maple, see "Smoothing Figured Wood."

2. Cut the sides to length, but leave them each at least ¼ in. wider than finished width. This will make routing the tails on the ends easier.

Cutting the dovetail slots

Consistency is the key with all sliding dovetail joints. If you start with flat stock of uniform thickness and length, the joinery will flow smoothly. If you don't, you're sure to get joints that are too tight at one end and loose at the other. As there isn't much else holding this shelf together, cutting these joints well is important.

1. Mill ample test pieces out of (non-curly maple) scrap to use before you commit the real pieces to the router bit.

2. Make a jig to cut the small dovetail slots in the sides. (see "Jig for Routing Dovetail Slots"). The jig is simply a piece of plywood with a ½-in. slot, a front fence to register the jig square to the edge of the workpiece, and a rear stop. In order for this jig to work

SMOOTHING FIGURED WOOD

Jointing figured wood such as curly maple can be tricky because of the wood's tendency to tear out. The grain doesn't run in one direction, so you can't choose a way to cut that's with the grain. There is, unfortunately, no foolproof strategy to cut curly grain, just a few pointers that will help.

First, the sharper your jointer and planer blades the better. Dull blades will have a much greater tendency to tear out, so if you haven't changed them in a while, do it now.

Second, take many very light cuts instead of fewer deep cuts.

Third, if you're using a handplane, skew it about 45 degrees in the cut. This will make the blade cut with a shearing action that doesn't tear out as much.

Fourth, try dampening the surface to be planed or joined. The water won't penetrate far, but it will create a layer of wet wood that cuts much more easily and won't tear out. Don't get the boards too wet or they'll warp and your planer will rust.

Jig for Routing Dovetail Slots

This plywood jig clamps to the workpiece and has a front fence and a slot that guides a router with a ³⁄₈" top-bearing dovetail bit. You can cut dovetail slots, dadoes, and other types of cross-grain cuts with it.

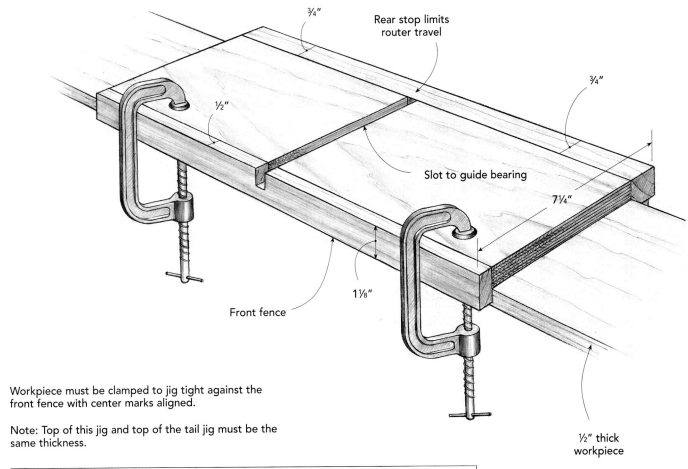

³⁄₄"

Rear stop limits router travel

³⁄₄"

½"

Slot to guide bearing

7¼"

Front fence

1⅛"

Workpiece must be clamped to jig tight against the front fence with center marks aligned.

Note: Top of this jig and top of the tail jig must be the same thickness.

½" thick workpiece

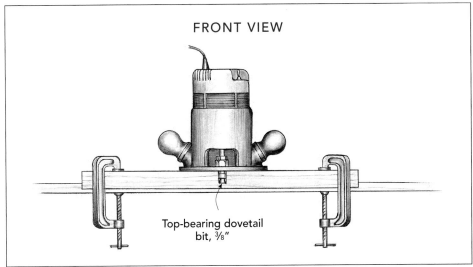

FRONT VIEW

Top-bearing dovetail bit, ³⁄₈"

Photo A: The dovetail slot jig clamps to the workpiece with the centerline on the jig and the workpiece lined up. The slot guides the bearing on the dovetail bit.

Photo B: The jig for routing tails holds the shelf vertical and cuts one side of the tail at a time. It is accurate, if a little fussy to set up.

with the jig for cutting the tails, the tops of each must be exactly the same thickness.

3. Mark the centerlines for each shelf on both side pieces and transfer them to the back edge. The centerline is used to line up a corresponding centerline on the jig.

4. Fit your router with a ⅜-in. dovetail bit with a ½-in. top bearing, and set it to cut halfway through the piece, in this case ¼ in. deep.

5. Clamp the jig to the workpiece with centerlines aligned and cut the slots (see **photo A**). Because these are very small slots, the router doesn't have to work hard to cut them, and the jig traps the bit so it can't wander. If you were cutting anything larger, you would remove some waste from the slot first with a small straight bit.

Cutting the tails on the shelves

Cutting the tails is not hard, just fussy to set up. This is where those scrap pieces you saved come into play.

Tip: If you rout the dovetail slots in the sides before you cut their profiles, you don't have to worry about tearout at the ends of the cuts.

1. Make a jig to cut the tails (see "Jig for Routing Tails").

2. Clamp a piece of scrap to the jig, making sure the end of the shelf is tight against the underside of the fence.

3. Adjust the fence to what you think is about right and cut one side of the tail.

4. Turn the piece around, reclamp it, and rout the other side.

5. Check the scrap piece's fit in the slot and make whatever adjustment is necessary to the fence. In this way, creep up on the correct fit. You will see why I call this fussy: The right fit comes down to minute fence adjustments, which can be maddening to get just right. Remember that each adjustment is doubled because you cut both sides of the tail.

6. Once the setting is correct, rout the tails on all the shelves (see **photo B**). Again, don't worry about tearout since the shelves are still wider than their finished width.

Jig for Routing Tails

This jig guides a router at 90 degrees to the end of a workpiece and will cut sliding dovetails quite well. It is built of ¾" plywood.

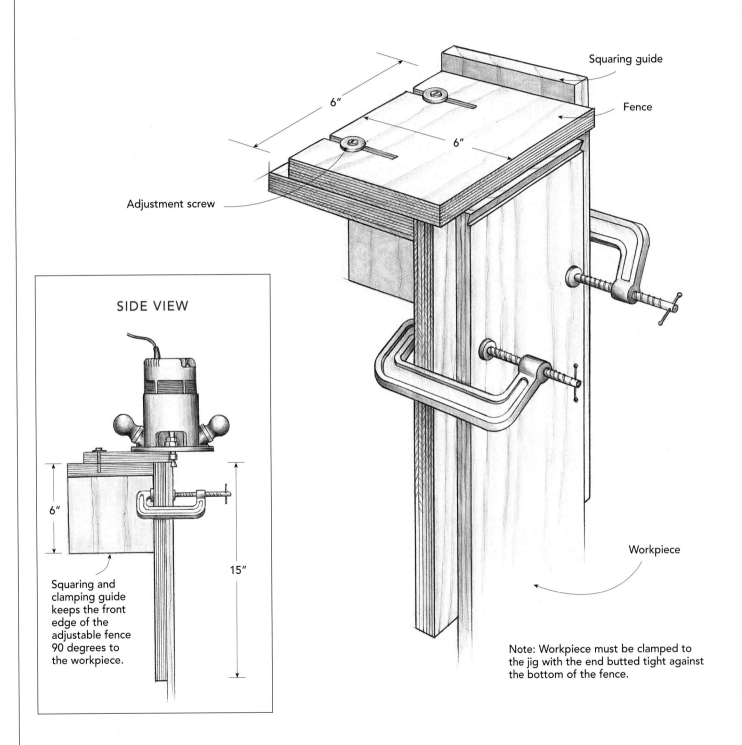

Squaring guide

Fence

6"

6"

Adjustment screw

SIDE VIEW

6"

15"

Squaring and clamping guide keeps the front edge of the adjustable fence 90 degrees to the workpiece.

Workpiece

Note: Workpiece must be clamped to the jig with the end butted tight against the bottom of the fence.

SHAPING THE SIDES AND SHELVES

Making and using a plywood pattern for the sides

Routing with a pattern to cut the profiles is useful on a number of counts. It ensures a perfect edge and makes both sides identical.

1. Either copy the profile provided or experiment with sketching different curves and angles until you find a profile you like.
2. Make a very precise plywood pattern of the finished shape of the sides.
3. Use a straightedge and a router with a flush-trimming bit for the straight taper and a stationary sander to true the curves. If you don't have a stationary sander, use files, rasps, and sanding blocks to smooth the curves.
4. With the pattern, trace the shape on both sides and cut them on a bandsaw as close as

you can to the line (see **photo C**). The less wood left, the less chance there is of tearout when you rout the finished shape.

Using the pattern to shape the sides

1. Attach the pattern to a side using double-sided tape.
2. With a ½-in. flush-trimming bit in the router table, rout the final shape (see **photo D**). Be careful to rout in an anti-climb cut to avoid injury to both self and workpiece (see "Routing the Right Way"). Take very light cuts to avoid tearout.

Cutting shelves to width

1. Rip a clean 90-degree edge on all the shelves, but not to finished width.
2. Rip the two bottom shelves to width, taking the measurements directly from the finished sides. Double ripping will remove any tearout from routing the tails.

Photo C: Rough out the profile of the sides on the bandsaw after you've cut the joinery. Try to cut as close to the line as possible without going over it.

Photo D: The plywood pattern helps you rout a smooth near-perfect edge on the profile of the sides.

ROUTING THE RIGHT WAY

Always run the workpiece against the rotation of the router bit. Otherwise it could pull the piece out of your hands or, worse, pull your hand into the bit. Technically, this is called anti-climb cutting. I call it the "right way," and it's much safer.

Tip: You can give the shelf several coats of oil, but what's the point? The most wear a shelf like this will get is from dusting!

3. Because the front edges of the top three shelves are angled to match the tapered sides, transfer the angle to your table saw and rip this angle on these shelves.

ASSEMBLY AND FINISHING

Gluing up

1. Sand all the pieces to 180 grit.
2. Slide each shelf halfway into its slot.
3. Carefully brush a little glue on the front of each tail and the back of each slot. It pays to be neat here. If the joints fit well, very little glue is needed. You don't want to be cleaning up a lot of glue on an otherwise finished piece.
4. Starting at the bottom, tap each shelf flush with the front, clamping across each shelf as you go (see **photo E**).

Applying the finish

Finish this piece with Antique Oil Finish made by Minwax. This is not a particularly hard-wearing oil, but it produces a nice finish. This oil also has just a hint of color to it, which helps bring out the figure in woods like curly or bird's-eye maple.

1. Flood the surface for the first coat and wait about 15 minutes before wiping off the excess.
2. Let the final coat dry at least a couple of hours, and then apply a second coat, wet sanding the wood with 320-grit wet-dry sandpaper.
3. Wipe off any excess again and rub the piece dry with a clean, soft cloth and let it dry overnight. That's it.

Photo E: Clamp one shelf in place at a time, as you go. The clamps don't make the subsequent shelf harder to tap home, and they can help make the shelf square overall.

Attaching the brass hangers

Peter Turner used hangers that were mortised into the back of the shelf. I used some that were surface-mounted, and had to place some clear bumpers on the back of my shelf that stick out as far as the screw heads to allow the shelf to lie flat against the wall. However, any reasonably attractive hanger will do just fine.

Standing
V-Shelf Bookcase

When I first saw the original of this bookcase, it reminded me of similar cases from my childhood and brought back a lot of memories. I can still see my father sitting in a large easy chair next to one of these V-shelves stuffed with books and magazines, a floor lamp shining across his face as he read. Reading was still something that everyone I knew enjoyed. Television was a novelty then, at least in my house. So with the romantic hope that I could inject some of that memory into my life (and banish my color TV), I decided to build this bookcase.

The design of this bookcase is from Peter Turner, a woodworker and furniture maker in Portland, Maine, who modeled it after one that belonged to his great-grandmother. It has V-shaped shelves, which cradle the books.

Turner made his shelf out of cherry; but I chose mahogany to achieve the darker, more subdued look and feel I remember. Also, I had a nice 6/4 mahogany board, large enough for the whole project, that I could resaw and book-match. Otherwise my V-shelf is essentially the same as Turner's.

It's a good style of bookcase to place between a chair and sofa in a living room because it's accessible from both sides, and it's difficult to knock the books out of it. It also has a flat bottom shelf for magazines, which would slither sideways if stored in the V-shelves.

V-Shelf Bookcase for Magazines and Books

WITH NO BACK, the bookshelf is accessible from both sides. The top V-shelf is smaller than the lower shelf, which is an appropriate size for larger books and also gives the bookshelf good proportions. The decorative cutouts on the sides give it some character. The tapered sides and shelves are made from ½" thick mahogany, joined with #10 biscuits.

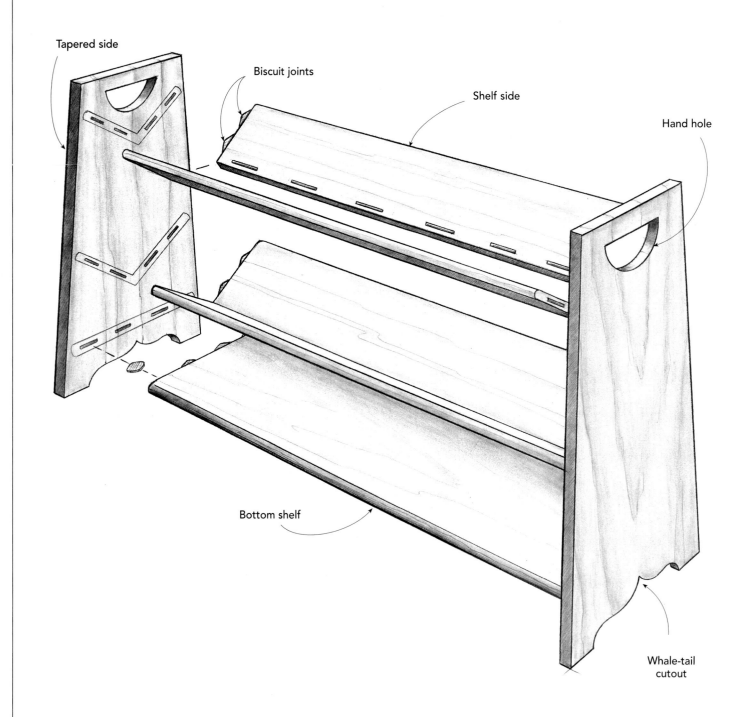

Tapered side

Biscuit joints

Shelf side

Hand hole

Bottom shelf

Whale-tail cutout

SIDE VIEW

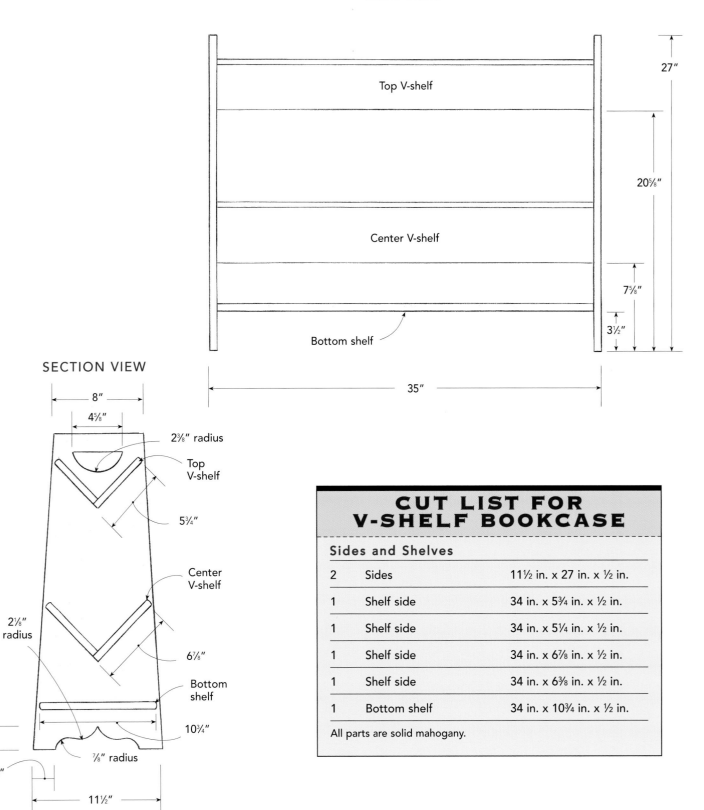

Top V-shelf

Center V-shelf

Bottom shelf

27"

20⅝"

7⅝"

3½"

35"

SECTION VIEW

8"

4⅝"

2⅜" radius

Top V-shelf

5¾"

Center V-shelf

2⅛" radius

6⅞"

Bottom shelf

2"

10¾"

⅞" radius

2"

11½"

CUT LIST FOR V-SHELF BOOKCASE

Sides and Shelves

2	Sides	11½ in. x 27 in. x ½ in.
1	Shelf side	34 in. x 5¾ in. x ½ in.
1	Shelf side	34 in. x 5¼ in. x ½ in.
1	Shelf side	34 in. x 6⅞ in. x ½ in.
1	Shelf side	34 in. x 6⅜ in. x ½ in.
1	Bottom shelf	34 in. x 10¾ in. x ½ in.

All parts are solid mahogany.

BUILDING THE BOOKCASE STEP-BY-STEP

THIS IS A SMALL, easy-to-build piece with a few simple design details. Using ½-in. solid wood gives the piece a lightness of style that would be lost with thicker boards. The whole bookcase is joined to-gether with biscuits, making the work flow fairly quickly. Spend the time to get the details just right, especially making the edge profiles nice and crisp.

> *Tip: It's best to plane parts to finished thickness after any edge-joining; but remember that you're limited by the width of your planer.*

SHAPING THE PARTS

Preparing the stock

Book-matching the sides and shelves adds a beautiful, though not really necessary, touch to the bookcase. I just happened to have the 6/4 lumber; I probably wouldn't have gone to the trouble to buy it.

1. Flatten, edge joint, and plane flat enough 8-in.- to 9-in.-wide 6/4 mahogany boards for all the parts.

TABLE-SAW TAPERING JIG

The angled stop positions the bottom of the work-piece at the correct 3-degree angle. The registration block is set on the jig 11½" from the line of cut, which is the width of the bottom of the finished side.

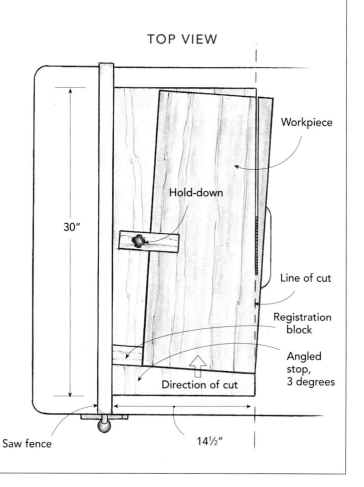

TOP VIEW

Workpiece

Hold-down

30"

Line of cut

Registration block

Angled stop, 3 degrees

Direction of cut

Saw fence

14½"

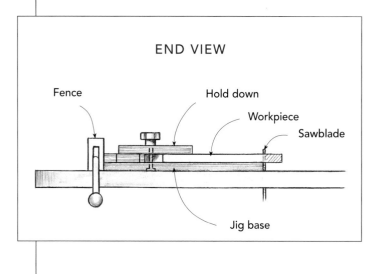

END VIEW

Fence

Hold down

Workpiece

Sawblade

Jig base

2. Resaw the boards on a bandsaw to half their thickness, about ⅝ in., and mark the pairs for the sides and shelves.

3. Plane down all the parts to ½-in.-thick finished stock.

4. If you don't have 6/4 lumber to work with, simply start with 4/4 stock and mill it to thickness. Try to get boards at least 7 in. wide, so you won't have to glue up stock for each half of the V-shelves.

Gluing up the sides

1. Choose the best book-matched boards for the sides. Glue and clamp up the pairs. Keep the glueline in the very center of the boards. Even if you're not book-matching, it will look best.

2. Snug up the clamps just enough to keep things together but still allow them to be moved a little. Slide or tap them even, and then tighten the clamps.

3. Pick the second-best book-matches for the V-shelves and set them aside.

4. Pick out boards to book-match for the bottom shelf last, since a poor match here will be hard to notice. Glue them up like the sides.

Cutting the parts to size

1. Sand the glue joints. Try not to sand too aggressively.

2. Rip all pieces to their final widths on the table saw. Remember that you have to take even amounts off both sides of the glued-up pieces. This will keep the glue joint centered in the finished piece.

3. To rip the V-shelf parts, place the mating edges of the boards together and rip ½ in. from the mating edge of what will be the narrower board.

4. Rip the V-shelf parts to their respective widths on the opposite edge. This will produce a perfectly book-matched face when this board overlaps the wider board to construct the V.

5. Cut the sides and shelves to finished length on a radial-arm saw or a table saw with a good miter gauge. All the shelf components must be square and exactly the same length.

Tapering the sides

1. To taper the edges of the sides, first build a taper jig (see "Table-Saw Tapering Jig").

2. Position the jig against the saw fence with the outer edge just touching the sawblade, and lock the fence in place.

3. Secure one of the sides in the jig against the angled stop and up against the registration block.

4. Run the whole assembly through the saw (see **photo A**).

5. Flip the piece over, secure it in the jig, and cut the taper on the other side of the side.

Tip: Be meticulous during glue-up since these boards are finished thickness. Any misalignment will have to be sanded out and cause your boards to vary in thickness—and there is no place to hide this on the piece.

Photo A: A simple taper jig cuts the angle on the side. With the registration block, it also ensures the sides are uniformly wide.

Photo B: A cardboard template with curves made by eye is used for scribing the whale-tail cutout. Use a jigsaw to cut away the waste.

Photo C: Smoothing the whale-tale detail can be accomplished with files, rasps, and an assortment of sandpaper and blocks.

ADDING DETAILS TO THE SIDES AND EDGES

Making the cutouts and shaping the edges

1. Mark out the hand holes with a compass and a straightedge.

2. Drill a large hole on the inside edge of the hole.

3. Using a jigsaw fitted with a fine blade, cut as close to the layout lines as possible.

4. Make a cardboard template to lay out half of the whale tail, since each side is a mirror image of the other. Use a compass or draw the shape by eye and adjust the curves until they look right. Cut out the template with a razor knife (see **photo B**).

5. Cut out the whale tail the same way you cut out the hand hole.

6. To smooth the cutouts, use a combination of rasps, files, and sandpaper-covered blocks and dowels (see **photo C**).

7. Ease the inside edges of the hand holes with a ¼-in. piloted roundover bit. Run it around the inside of the cutouts from both sides.

8. Work with a file and some sandpaper to shape the corners that the router bit can't reach.

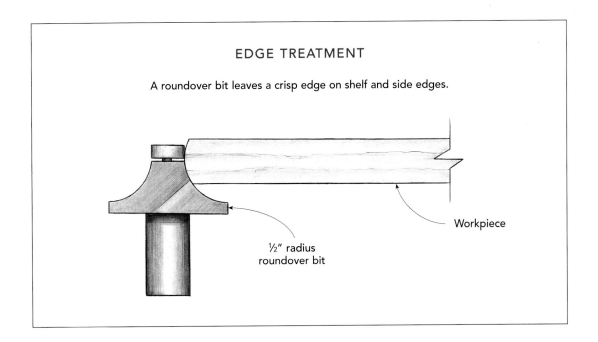

EDGE TREATMENT

A roundover bit leaves a crisp edge on shelf and side edges.

½" radius
roundover bit

Workpiece

Shaping the shelf edges

The long edges of both V-shelves and all edges of the sides should be rounded over. But keep in mind that the roundover looks best when you leave a crisp edge where it meets the edge of the board.

1. Set a ½-in.-radius roundover bit in a router table with the bearing higher than the center of the board and so that the blade cuts to the center (see "Edge Treatment").

2. Cut both sides of each board to produce a rounded edge.

CUTTING THE JOINERY

Joining V-shelves

The shelf sides are set against each other at 90 degrees, so there's nothing really special or difficult about this joint.

1. Orient the V-shelf boards correctly for a book-match. It's easy to forget which boards go together.

2. Take the narrower board from each set, and cut #10 biscuit slots in the edge.

3. Cut the corresponding slots in the faces of the opposite board.

HOW MANY BISCUITS IN A GOOD EDGE JOINT?

The number of biscuits to use on a given edge depends on a number of factors and what jobs they're being asked to perform.

For most edge-joint applications, space biscuits between 4 in. and 6 in. apart. If the biscuits are for alignment only and the boards are flat and not prone to warping, I would space them farther apart.

If the wood is not especially flat or prone to warping, bring the biscuits closer together. And if you're concerned about the strength of the joint, add biscuits. There's some debate on how much strength biscuits add to an edge joint (after all, most glues are harder to break than the wood itself in some directions); but I figure a few more biscuits can't hurt.

Photo D: Cut biscuit slots in the edges of the narrower pieces and the faces of the wider pieces. When gluing, put a clamp over each biscuit for even pressure.

Photo E: Cut four biscuits in the end of each V-shelf, registering the joiner off the shelf backs. Leave the layout lines.

Tip: Orient the biscuits in the edge of the thin board and on the face of the wider board so that the V-shelf has equal-width sides when joined (the longer one tucks under the short one).

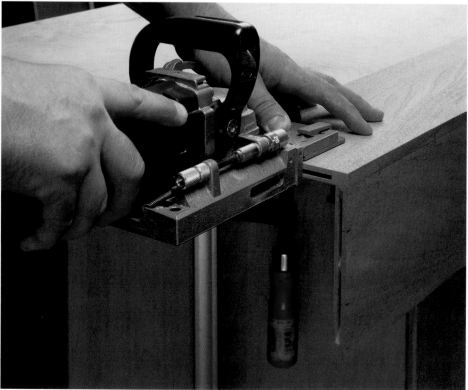

4. Glue and clamp the pairs, making sure the clamping pressure doesn't throw the assembly out of square. Use one clamp at each biscuit location and one at each end (see **photo D**).

5. Check to make sure that the ends of both shelf assemblies are exactly even. This joint forms the structure of the whole piece, and it's very visible. It would be very difficult to recut the ends of the shelves to fix any misalignment problems after they are glued together.

Attaching the shelves to the sides

1. Cut four biscuit slots on the ends of each shelf and leave the layout lines. Cut the slots with the fence registering against the bottom of the shelves (see **photo E**).

2. Draw a vertical centerline on the inside face of each side.

3. To locate a V-shelf, place it on end against a side, keeping the apex of the V on the centerline, and move it along the centerline until both edges are inset ⅛ in. from the case side. (see "Shelf Location").

4. Hold the shelf in place and trace along the bottom edge with a pencil (see **photo F**).

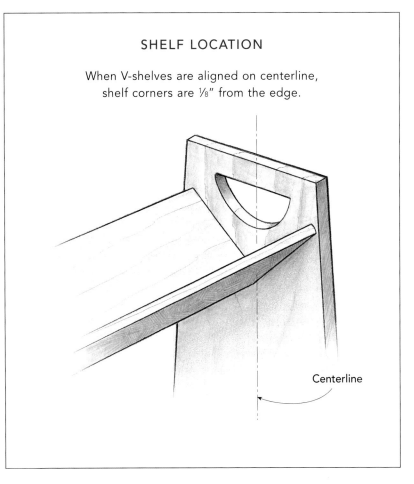

SHELF LOCATION

When V-shelves are aligned on centerline, shelf corners are ⅛" from the edge.

Centerline

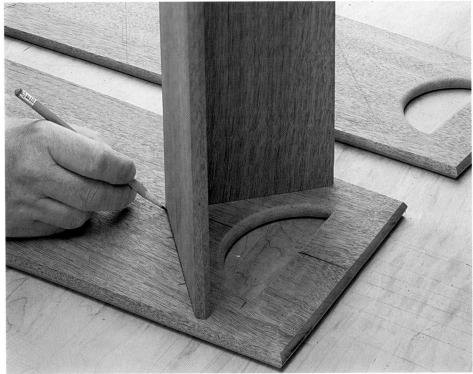

Photo F: Use the assembled V-shelves as marking guides. Scribe a line around the bottom of the shelf to help you align the biscuit joiner in the cut.

5. Transfer the reference lines for the biscuit slots.

6. To determine how to align the biscuit joiner on the face of the side, draw a line parallel to the line scribed around the shelf bottom that will align the joiner in the right place. The location of this line depends on the distance between your biscuit joiner base and the blade.

For example, my biscuit joiner is designed to cut a slot centered ⅜ in. away from the base, which is too high for ½-in.-thick shelves. The adapter plate for cutting shallow biscuits has a marking gauge built into it for this purpose (see **photo G**). If your machine doesn't, scribe a line at whatever distance is best.

7. Make a plywood fence for the biscuit joiner with index marks for the slot locations and centerline.

8. Lay this fence along the reference line, then place the biscuit joiner against it and cut the slots (see **photo H**).

ASSEMBLY AND FINISHING

Glue-up

1. Before final assembly, sand all the parts to 180 grit and dry-fit the piece.

2. Check if the V-shelves are flush and square at their ends and make any necessary minor adjustments with a low-angle block plane.

Photo H: A ¾-in.-thick scrap of plywood aligned on the reference line makes an excellent guide for the biscuit joiner when making the V-shelf cuts.

3. How you glue and clamp up the piece will depend on the type of clamps you have, but you will find out what you need during the dry-fit stage.

4. Use an additional caul to close up the apex of the bottom V-shelf if it doesn't go together just right.

5. Keep a square on hand to periodically check for square and adjust clamps if necessary.

Applying the finish

I used Sutherland Welles Polymerized Tung Oil, Medium Luster (see Sources on pp. 182-183). It is a relatively difficult oil to apply correctly (make sure you follow the directions on the can), but I recommend it highly.

Peter Turner used Bioshield Hard Oil #9 finish. It is a linseed oil-based product that contains citrus solvents. The oil is available from the Eco Design Company through the Natural Choice (see Sources). Peter prefers these products because of their low toxicity, nice satin sheen, and pleasant lemony scent.

Tip: It's easiest to glue and clamp the piece when it's standing upright on its feet. In this position, you can place clamps on most of the joints by using the hand holes and the whale-tail cutouts.

COUNTRY COLONIAL BOOKCASE

I based this bookcase on one built by Randy O'Donnell, a period-furniture maker who lives in the countryside near Bloomington, Indiana. Randy normally builds rather complex formal reproductions of 18th-century furniture ranging from William and Mary style to Federal style.

You might wonder, as I did, how he came to build what he describes as a simple country piece. Randy's wife, Susy, crafts and sells spongeware, a type of stoneware used as the inexpensive "everyday" dishes in 19th-century homes. She and Randy sometimes show their respective work together. So they needed a case to display the 19th-century stoneware at its best in a space otherwise occupied by 18th-century formal furniture.

The result is a timeless design with strong 18th-century American roots. The inspiration for the curved work comes from a reproduction of an early 18th-century bucket bench that Randy saw in a book of plans. Bucket benches are cases that held water buckets before homes had running water. The bench had scrolled positive and negative shapes at its crown and base, and corner base cutouts that resemble bracket feet, which Randy adapted for this bookcase.

The open back and small scale (it's just over 5 ft. tall) give this bookcase a light feeling. It has a presence that is at once casual and formal.

Country Colonial Bookcase

THIS COUNTRY-STYLE open bookcase is made of clear pine, joined with dadoes and cut nails. The decorative scrollwork and the profiled sides make for a visually stimulating piece. It's well suited for open display space—crowding it would hide the scrollwork.

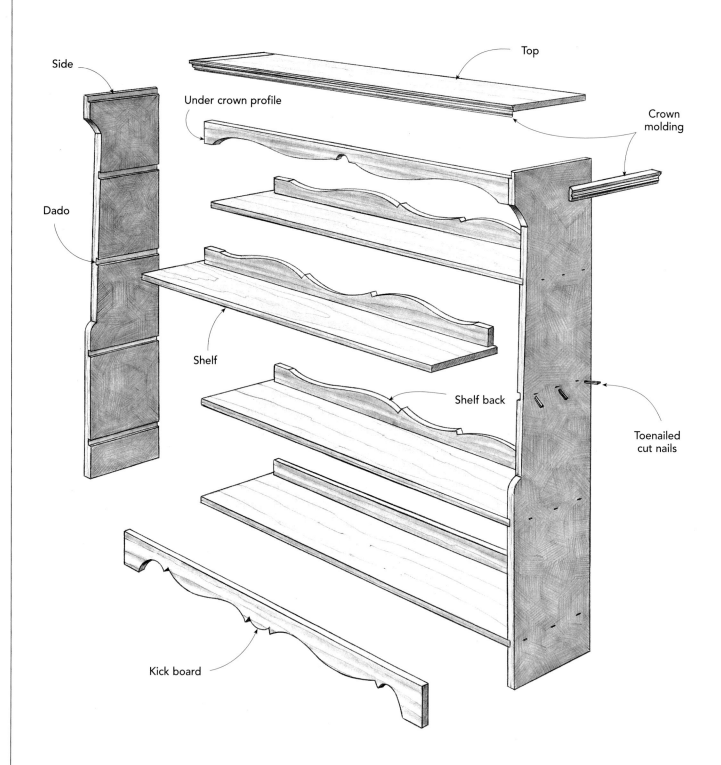

Side

Under crown profile

Dado

Shelf

Top

Crown molding

Shelf back

Toenailed cut nails

Kick board

FRONT VIEW

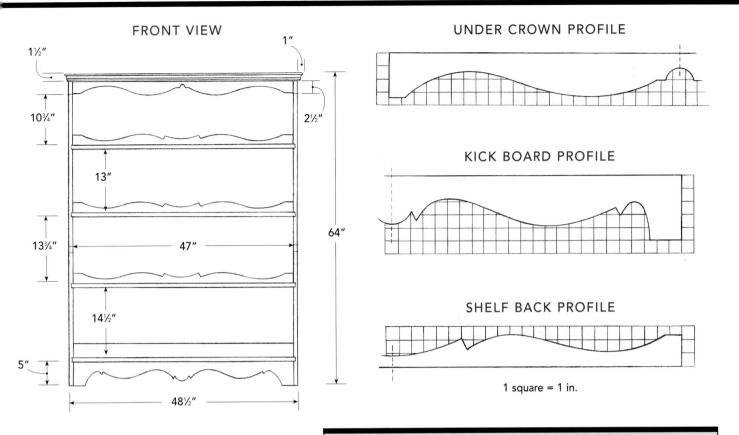

1½"

1"

10¾"

2½"

13"

13¾"

47"

64"

14½"

5"

48½"

UNDER CROWN PROFILE

KICK BOARD PROFILE

SHELF BACK PROFILE

1 square = 1 in.

SIDE VIEW

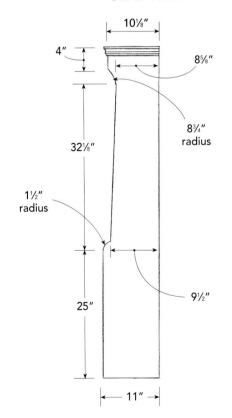

10⅛"

4"

8⅝"

8¾" radius

32⅛"

1½" radius

9½"

25"

11"

BUILDING THE BOOKCASE STEP-BY-STEP

ALTHOUGH THIS BOOKCASE takes a bit of time to build, details such as its stepped tapered sides, decorative cutouts, and cut nails make it a fun and interesting project. And the painted finish on this piece is particularly intriguing. With several layers of milk paint and a crackle finish, it may well expand your finishing repertoire. The use of softwood in its construction also makes it a natural for honing your hand-tool skills.

Tip: Make sure all the shelves are the same thickness. This is important because the dadoes are cut to hold the full thickness of the shelves. All the other parts can have minor differences without affecting the fit of the piece.

MAKING AND ASSEMBLING THE CASE

Preparing the stock

1. Draw up a cut list for all the lumber you'll need.
2. Mill up the stock, or if you use presurfaced stock, check that all your boards are flat and straight (see "Using Presurfaced Lumber"). If the presurfaced boards you buy are not quite the same thickness, take a light pass on each side through a planer or a thickness sander.
3. Sand the faces smooth.
4. Crosscut the sides and shelves to finished length. Leave all the rest of the stock, including the top of the case, at full length and width for now.

Cutting the dadoes in the sides

It's easiest to lay out and cut dadoes for the shelves in the sides before the front edge is shaped. This way, all your reference surfaces are still square.

1. Clamp the two sides together, back edge to back edge, with their inside faces up. Make sure the faces are flush with each other and that the ends line up exactly.
2. Lay out the dadoes to the thickness of the shelves and rout them with an aluminum guide or another fence clamped at a right angle to the edge of the sides.

USING PRESURFACED LUMBER

You can build very nice things from lumberyard or home-center wood (if you didn't already know). You just need to choose carefully.

I built this bookcase from 1-in. by 12-in. D-select, or clear pine. It's the most expensive of the trim material available at my lumberyard, but it's the best quality. This grade has few if any knots. In the 12-in. widths, it tends to be straightest and flattest. Narrower stock, even in this select grade, seems generally to be of lesser quality. So I chose to cut all the parts, including the narrower ones, from the 12-in.-wide stock.

As quality still varies from board to board, I made sure to pick through the boards. I sight down the whole length for extreme flatness and consistent thickness. Sometimes commercially milled boards are slightly uneven in thickness; the variations are unimportant to a builder, but perhaps not so to a furniture maker. Taking a light pass on each side through a planer or a thickness sander can be a good idea.

I should point out for those who may not know that in lumberyard lingo a 1-in. by 12-in. board has actual dimensions of ¾ in. by 11¼ in. Construction material like this is always labeled with the dimensions of the rough stock before planing (which is why a 2x4 is really 1½ in. by 3½ in.).

Tip: When jigsaw-ing the various shaped parts of this bookcase, cut right to the line with a fine blade. This type of pine is very soft, and the jigsaw won't wander much in the cut. The fine blade leaves a sur-face that needs little cleanup.

Photo A: Rout the dadoes for the shelves in the sides with the sides clamped back edge to back edge.

3. Make two overlapping passes with a ½-in. straight bit set to approximately ⅜ in. deep, or half the thickness of the sides (see **photo A**).
4. Leave the dadoes just slightly shy of full width. This allows you to make any minor adjustments necessary to fit the shelves by sanding them.

Tearout at the ends of the cuts is not an issue because you'll trim ⅛ in. off each side later to bring the boards to the finished width of 11 in.

Tapering and shaping the sides

The upper half of the bookcase sides has a distinctive profile. About 25 in. up from the floor the sides step back, and they taper slightly toward the top before coming forward again to 10⅛ in. wide at the crown.

1. Take the measurements for the profiles from the drawings on pp. 70-71 and lay out the profiles on the sides. They do not need to be exactly the same.
2. Cut the profiles with a jigsaw fitted with a fine blade (see **photo B**).

Photo B: Use a jigsaw to cut the profiles in the front edges of the sides. These pieces are too large to cut comfortably on a bandsaw.

Photo C: Alternate the angle of the nails into the shelf ends to give the joint greater strength and to prevent them from pulling apart.

Tip: If you're going to apply a clear finish to the bookcase, sand the sides before you nail the shelves in place. Otherwise, you'll sand the proud heads of the nails, removing their black finish.

3. Clamp the two sides together, profile to profile, and flush at the top, bottom, and back.

4. With a combination of machine and hand-sanding, clean up both profiles at the same time. This allows you to save time, match the two profiles, and prevent rounding the soft edges.

Cutting the shelves to width

1. Measure the width, front to back, of all the dadoes.

2. Transfer these measurements to the shelves.

3. Rip the bottom two shelves to just slightly more than the width. You'll trim them flush when they're installed.

4. The top two shelves intersect the sides at their tapered edges. Use a bevel gauge to transfer the angle to the table saw, and rip these shelves to width at that angle plus a little extra.

Assembling the case

1. Check the fit of the shelves in their dadoes. Sand to fit any shelves that are too tight.

2. Finish-sand the shelves and the inside of the sides.

3. With the sides lying inside-face up on the bench (or on a blanket on the floor), spread glue into all the dadoes.

4. Position the shelves in the dadoes of one side, keeping them flush with the back edge and slightly proud of the front edge.

5. Lay the other side on top of the opposite ends of the shelves and apply clamps at each shelf, front and back, side to side.

6. Check that the shelves are seated across the width of the joints. Some cauls may be necessary to apply pressure to the center of the joints.

7. Measure across the diagonals to make sure you're not assembling a parallelogram-shaped bookcase.

8. Also measure across the case at one of the shelf locations to get the overall width of the piece.

9. Take this measurement and crosscut the top to this length.

10. Rip the top to 10⅛ in. wide.

11. Biscuit the top to the sides.

12. When the glue is dry, remove the clamps and sand the outside of the case.

13. Nail all the joints with 2-in.-long reproduction cut nails from Whitechapel (see Sources on pp. 182-183). Use three nails per joint, alternately toenailed or angled into the joint (see **photo C**). Toenailing strengthens the joint by making it harder for the nails to pull out and hence to pull the joint apart.

14. Leave the nail heads proud of the surface.

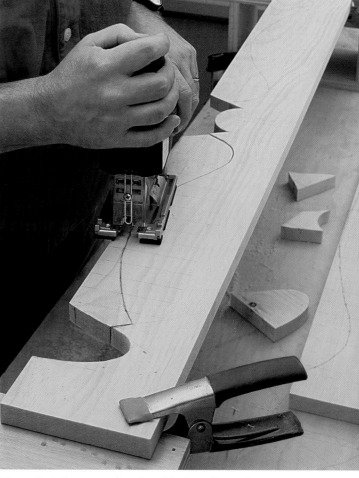

Photo D: Transfer distances from the half of the profile you draw by hand to the other half in short increments. Then simply connect the dots to create a mirror image of the profile.

Photo E: A jigsaw with a fine blade will cut the profiles cleanly.

MAKING THE DECORATIVE MEMBERS

Laying out the profiles

Certainly the most time-consuming task in making this bookcase is cutting the decorative members on the back of the shelves, under the crown, and at the base.

1. Either photocopy and enlarge the profiles from the drawings on pp. 70-71, or sketch them by hand. This option isn't as hard or random as it may seem. It just takes patience.
2. Crosscut the members to length, first measuring between the sides at each location. Rip the parts to their respective widths.

3. To lay out the symmetrical profile (or any profile) by hand, draw half of the shape directly on the workpiece from the centerline out to the edge. Erase and redraw as needed.
4. Divide the workpiece along its entire length into ½-in. sections and draw lines across the piece intersecting with the drawn profile.
5. Measure up from the bottom edge of the board to the point of each intersection and transfer these measurements to the corresponding lines on the other half of the board.
6. Connect these points to create the matching half of the shape. You'll be surprised how well it works (see **photo D**).

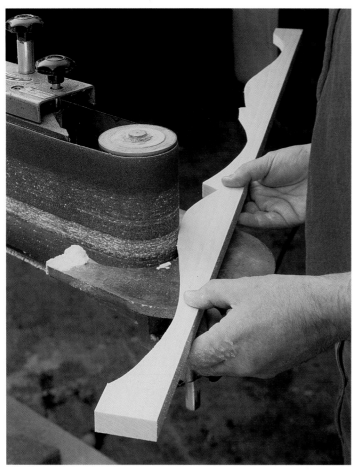

Photo F: A stationary sander does a good job on the larger profiles. Smaller profiles have to be worked with smaller sanders and by hand sanding.

Photo G: Position and glue the decorative members flush with the back edge of the shelf and nail in from the sides.

Tip: Don't connect the two molding profiles before attaching them to the case. They're easier to attach separately.

Cutting and installing the members

1. Cut out these shapes with a jigsaw fitted with a fine blade, getting as close to the line as possible without cutting over them (see **photo E** on p. 75).

2. Clean up the larger curves on a stationary sander or with a belt sander clamped in a vise (see **photo F**). Then move to a small random-orbit sander. Finally, hand-sand the smaller profiles.

3. Glue and clamp the pieces into their respective locations, driving cut nails through the sides of the case and into their ends (see **photo G**).

4. Cut the straight board for the back of the bottom shelf to size, and install it the same way as the others.

Shaping and installing the crown molding

Unless you have a special shaper cutter to mill the profile of the crown molding, you'll need to use a combination of router bits to produce this profile in two parts.

1. Rip and plane two 78-in.-long pieces of pine, one 1 in. by $^{15}/_{16}$ in. and the other ¾ in. by ⅝ in.

2. Cut the profiles on the pieces (see "Sequence of Cuts for Crown Molding"). It's necessary to mill these pieces from oversize stock because the router-bit bearing needs a surface to register against.

Sequence of Cuts for Crown Molding

Complex moldings are very simple to cut when broken down into steps.

SHAPING THE PARTS

1. Cut the cove with a ½" cove bit (see A).
2. Cut the bead in the bottom piece blank with a ¼" beading bit (see B).
3. Remove the waste from the face of the bottom piece on the table saw (see C).
4. Plane the top of the bottom piece to finished thickness (see D).
5. Block-plane the chamfer after the molding is installed.

FINISHED MOLDING

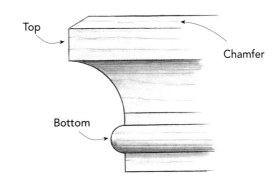

Top

Chamfer

Bottom

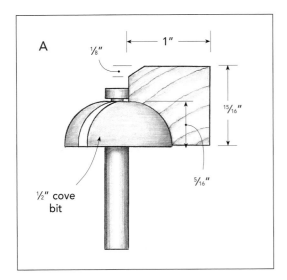

A

1"

⅛"

¹⁵⁄₁₆"

⁵⁄₁₆"

½" cove bit

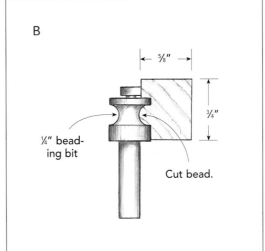

B

⁵⁄₈"

¾"

¼" bead-ing bit

Cut bead.

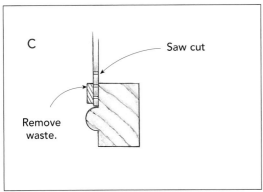

C

Saw cut

Remove waste.

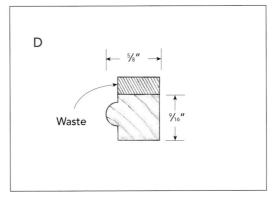

D

⁵⁄₈"

⁹⁄₁₆"

Waste

Photo H: Apply the crown molding, one piece at a time, with reproduction finish nails.

3. Miter one end of the larger piece and place it on the case with that miter lined up with one corner, mark the opposite corner, and cut that miter.

4. Apply a little glue to the molding and nail it in place using reproduction fine finish nails, available from Van Dyke Restorers (see Sources on pp. 182-183) (see **photo H**).

5. Divide the remaining piece of that molding in two and miter one end of each piece, one for the left side and one for the right side.

6. Hold these pieces in place, mark the rear edge of the molding at the back of the case, and trim them to length.

7. Because these pieces run across the grain of the sides, glue only the miter and nail them in place. The nails will hold this molding in place and still allow the side to move season-

ally without dislodging the molding or splitting the side.

8. Install the lower half of the crown using the same method. This is contrary to the advice I give for applying the molding to the Shaker-Style Bookcase (see pp. 46-55), but with the soft pine and the fairly narrow width of the top, I think it should work fine.

FINISHING UP

Trimming the shelves flush with the sides

1. With the piece assembled and all the decorative elements applied, trim the front edges of the shelves flush with a sharp block plane (see **photo I**).

Photo I: After installation, trim the front of each shelf flush with a sharp block plane.

2. Last, but not least, put a small chamfer around the top front edge of the crown, again using a block plane.

3. Finish-sand the entire piece to 180 grit and break all the corners. This is primarily handwork, but it goes fast on a softwood such as pine.

Applying the finish

Since I liked the finish and color of Randy O'Donnell's piece, I asked him what type of paint he used. At Randy's suggestion, I used a four-part milk-paint process. The finish attempts to give the impression that the piece has been painted a number of times.

1. Apply a coat of "Oyster White" milk paint. This is primarily a base or primer coat.

2. When it dries, follow it with a coat of "Pitch Black."

3. Apply a product called Antique Crackle, following the instructions given. This mimics the natural aging of paint and does what its name suggests. You can control the amount of crackle, depending on your taste. I made it subdued. The black undercoat shows through in very light streaks here and there and darkens the following red coat just a bit.

4. Give the bookcase a top coat of "Salem Red." All of these milk paints are available from the Old Fashioned Milk Paint Company (see Sources on pp. 182-183).

TRAPEZOIDAL BOOKCASE

I don't think I've ever built a perfect reproduction. Even when I really like an existing design, I need the piece to be slightly larger, I prefer some technique over one used in the original construction, or I don't have the exact materials. In any case, I think that one of the more enjoyable aspects of woodworking is trying new ideas and combinations. So it is with this bookcase, and twice over.

I based the design of this bookcase on one made by David Fay, a furniture maker in Oakland, California, who based his design on a turn-of-the-century Roycroft magazine pedestal. David's version strayed from the original somewhat, and my design strays from David's. The results are three versions of the same bookcase, with an overall look in common.

As is the case with much Arts and Crafts furniture, the essential decorative elements of all versions of this piece are the construction details, including the canted sides for stability and the wedged, locking through-tenons. In his interpretation of the original, David left these elements intact, but he omitted the molded crown and used cherry (instead of fumed white oak) and contrasting panga panga wood wedges and shelf supports.

My bookcase is identical to David's, but I used ash with zebrawood for the wedges. I also made mine knockdown for transporting.

Trapezoidal Knockdown Bookcase

THIS IS AN UPDATED, KNOCKDOWN VERSION of a Roycroft magazine stand held together with through wedge tenons on the top and bottom shelves. The middle shelves are held in position with unglued biscuits. The front edges of the sides are tapered 3 degrees, and the sides also lean toward each other at 3 degrees, giving the piece a trapezoidal shape.

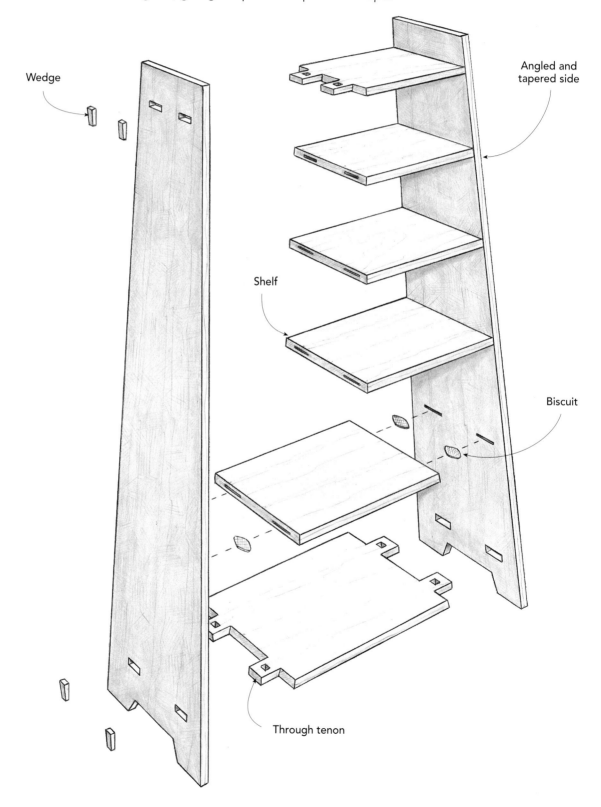

Wedge

Angled and tapered side

Shelf

Biscuit

Through tenon

FRONT VIEW

SIDE VIEW

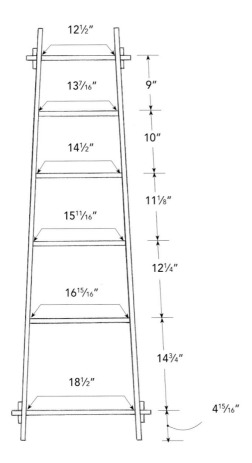

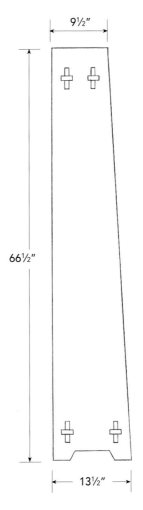

12½"

13⁷/₁₆"   9"

10"

14½"

11⅛"

15¹¹/₁₆"

12¼"

16¹⁵/₁₆"

14¾"

18½"

4¹⁵/₁₆"

9½"

66½"

13½"

Sides and shelves are ¾" thick.

CUT LIST FOR TRAPEZOIDAL BOOKCASE

Carcase and Shelves

2	Sides	13½ in. x 66⅝ in. x ¾ in.
1	Shelf	13⁷/₁₆ in. x 10⁵/₁₆ in. x ¾ in.
1	Shelf	14½ in. x 10¹⁵/₁₆ in. x ¾ in.
1	Shelf	15¹¹/₁₆ in. x 11⁹/₁₆ in. x ¾ in.
1	Shelf	16¹⁵/₁₆ in. x 12⁵/₁₆ in. x ¾ in.
1	Top shelf	17½ in. x 9¾ in. x ¾ in.
1	Bottom shelf	23½ in. x 13¼ in. x ¾ in.
8	Wedges	3⅜ in. x ¾ in. x ¾ in.

All parts are made of solid ash except for the zebrawood wedges.

BUILDING THE BOOKCASE STEP-BY-STEP

THIS BOOKCASE would be a cinch to build except for the 3-degree trapezoidal shape. All of the joinery must be cut at this angle, often with special-made jigs. The best place to begin is with a full-sized drawing of the bookcase (front and side views) on a good-quality light-colored plywood. It will be an excellent and accurate reference throughout the whole building process (see "Full-Scale Drawings").

MAKING THE SIDES AND SHELVES

Gluing up the stock

The smallest shelf is 9¾ in. deep, and the base of the sides is 13½ in. Unless you have access to some wide ash, you'll have to make the shelves and sides from two pieces.

FULL-SCALE DRAWINGS

Full-scale drawings may seem like overkill, but they are tremendously useful, especially when the piece is complex.

An accurate full-scale drawing lets you take all your measurements from it as you work. You don't have to fiddle with cut lists and calculate joints and details in your head. Just put a ruler on the drawing, and you have your measurement.

They're also helpful to visually evaluate the size and proportions of the piece. If you want to adapt a design to a different space or to hold some specific objects, the full-scale drawing helps you see what it will look like. Scale drawings can tell you only so much. Subtle changes that would be all but invisible in a small drawing can be quite dramatic full size.

To transfer angles from the drawing to a workpiece or machine, use a large protractor gauge, such as one made by CCKL Creator (available from Lee Valley Tools). It is much larger than a standard bevel gauge, and it allows a greater reach on the drawing and greater accuracy. It also allows you to read the actual angle. This makes resetting it a cinch, which isn't necessarily the case with a standard bevel gauge.

Photo A: The bookcase sides and shelves are wide (9½ in. to 13½ in.), and have to be glued up from two or more pieces.

1. If you can, resaw 8/4 stock for the sides and book-match them. I couldn't book-match the bookcase you see in the photos with the ash I had, but it is certainly worth the trouble.
2. If you use unmatched boards, choose the best match of grain and color for the sides, and decide if you want the glue joint parallel with the straight back or with the tapered edge on the front. I chose parallel to the back, which seemed the least obvious.
3. Glue up all the stock for the bookcase shelves and sides at once (see **photo A**).

Beveling ends and tapering sides

1. Cut the sides to length, but not at 90 degrees. The sides lean inward toward each other at 3 degrees, so crosscut the top and bottom edges at 93 degrees to the floor (or 87 degrees, depending from which direction you measure). This way when the bookcase sits on the floor, the bottom sits flat and the top edges are horizontal. Make sure the edges are parallel when finished.
2. The front edge of the bookcase has a taper (though the back does not). Lay it out by measuring from the back edge of each side 13½ in. at the bottom and 9½ in. at the top. Then draw a line between the marks.
3. Cut the taper along the line. I use a Festo circular saw that has a straightedge guide that's great for this kind of cut. It leaves a very smooth and straight edge (see **photo B**). The taper can also be rough-cut with a jigsaw and cleaned up with a straightedge and a router.
4. Cut the top and bottom shelf blanks a little wider than necessary and 3½ in. longer than the outside width of the case at their locations. This allows for the through tenons.
5. Later, after these shelves are installed, mark the exact depth from the sides, then rip a 3-degree bevel on the front edge. Then rip the back edge at 90 degrees.

Photo B: A circular saw and straightedge guide make cutting the tapers on the sides a cinch.

JOINERY

Cutting the mortises

The mortises that are used to join the top and bottom shelves to the sides are the trickiest part of this piece because they are angled and have to be cut cleanly to within a very close tolerance—as does all the joinery in this piece—because it all shows.

1. Make two router jigs, a right-handed one and a left-handed one, to cut the four mortises in the sides at a 3-degree angle (see "Jig for Routing Angled Mortises" on p. 86).
2. Attach the alignment fence to the left-handed jig on the angled edge. It is now set up to cut the mortises on the front edge of the left side.
3. Position the jig flush with the top and front edges on the outside face of the left side.

Tip: Standard bevel gauges should be set once and left set until you've finished with every similar angle. However, to give memory to a bevel gauge, trace the whole blade of the bevel gauge on a scrap of plywood.

Jigs for Routing Angled Mortises

To cut the four mortises in the sides, you need two jigs with movable fences. The jigs are identical except that they are mirror images of each other. One edge of each jig is angled like the front edge of the bookcase, and the bottoms of each are shimmed at 3 degrees, the same angle that the bookcase sides lean inward.

Jigs sit in the corners of their respective sides, and register off the edges to locate the mortises.

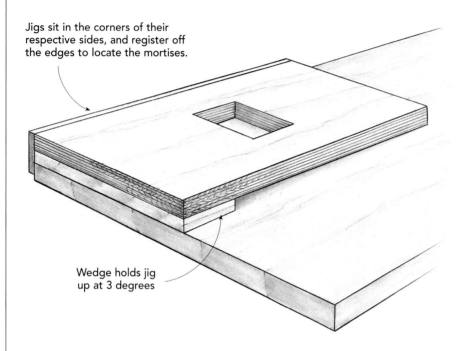

Wedge holds jig up at 3 degrees

LEFT-SIDE JIG

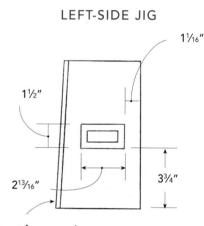

1 1/16"

1 1/2"

2 13/16"

3 3/4"

Alignment fence can be moved from front to back edge of jig for corresponding location on bookcase side.

RIGHT-SIDE JIG

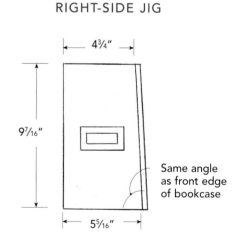

4 3/4"

9 7/16"

5 5/16"

Same angle as front edge of bookcase

JIG IN USE

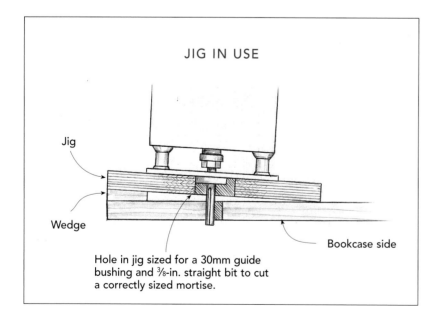

Jig

Wedge

Hole in jig sized for a 30mm guide bushing and 3/8-in. straight bit to cut a correctly sized mortise.

Bookcase side

Tip: Attach the jig to the workpiece with double-sided tape rather than clamps because they can get in the way of the router.

Photo C: To cut the through mortises in the sides, you need a left-handed and a right-handed router jig.

Photo D: The mortising jig tilts the router 3 degrees and cuts the mortise walls at the same angle.

4. Back up the cut on the underside with some scrap wood. Don't risk any tearout since everything shows.

5. Cut the upper mortises on the front edge of the left side with a plunge router. Advance the depth of cut in very small increments.

6. Slide the jig down the same side until it is flush with the bottom, and cut the bottom mortise on the same side (see **photo C**).

7. Take the alignment fence off the jig and attach it to the opposite side of the jig.

8. Move the jig to the back side and repeat the process for the back mortises (see **photo D**).

9. Square up the rounded mortise corners with a sharp chisel (see **photo E**).

10. Repeat this process on the other side of the bookcase but with the other jig.

Photo E: Square up the routed mortises with a sharp chisel.

Cut Sequence for Tenons

A support box attached to a crosscut sled makes a stable platform to cut tenons.
A stop block lets you angle the workpiece.

STEP 1: CUT CHEEKS

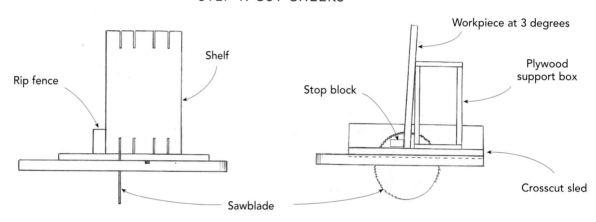

Rip fence

Shelf

Sawblade

Workpiece at 3 degrees

Stop block

Plywood support box

Crosscut sled

STEP 2: CUT SHOULDERS

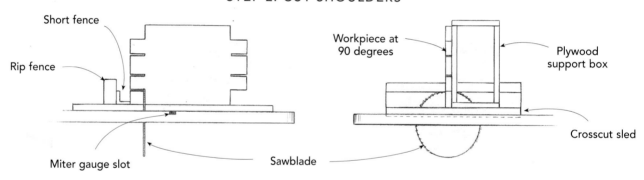

Short fence

Rip fence

Miter gauge slot

Sawblade

Workpiece at 90 degrees

Plywood support box

Crosscut sled

STEP 3: REMOVE CENTER PORTION

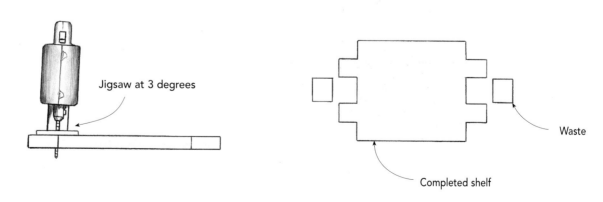

Jigsaw at 3 degrees

Waste

Completed shelf

Cutting the tenons in the top and bottom shelves

Choosing one method of tenoning over another is usually based on experience and machinery. I use my table saw because I'm comfortable with this machine and it produces a cut that requires the least amount of cleanup. However, feel free to cut the tenons as you like.

1. Attach a tall fence (actually a plywood box) to your table-saw crosscut sled at right angles to the blade.

2. Attach a stop block to the sled, in front of and parallel to the fence. This stop block is positioned to catch the edge of the workpiece that, when leaned back against the fence, is at 3 degrees to the top of the saw (see "Cut Sequence for Tenons").

3. Use the saw fence to position the cut, and raise the blade to a height that corresponds to the length of the tenon.

4. Push the sled across the blade to cut what are essentially the cheeks of the tenons (see **photo F**).

5. To cut the tenon shoulders, use the same jig, but with the stop block removed and the box fence pivoted 3 degrees relative to the sawblade (see **photo G**).

Photo F: A simple table-saw jig positions the workpiece to cut the angled cheeks of the tenons.

6. Place a short fence against the rip fence to position the cut and allow the cutoff to fall clear of the blade and fence.

7. Hold the workpiece against the fence (90 degrees to the saw table and 3 degrees to the blade).

8. With the sawblade just high enough to connect with the previous cut, push the sled across the blade, making the shoulder cuts.

9. Cut out the center portion with a jigsaw, with the blade set at 3 degrees.

Photo G: To cut the outside tenon shoulders, reposition the box fence 3 degrees to the blade.

Photo H: Clean up the jigsaw cut with a chisel.

Photo I: A hollow-chisel mortiser with a ⅜-in. bit is fast and accurate for cutting the mortises for the wedge.

10. Pare to the layout lines on each side with a sharp chisel, making sure to maintain the 3-degree angle across the shoulder (see **photo H** on p. 89).

Cutting the mortises in the tenons for the wedges

In a perfect world, the wedges would be simple to fit in the tenons, needing only accurate measurements and layout. In reality, there is a lot of fitting to get the wedges just right. Differences in the size of the mortise as little as $\frac{1}{32}$ in. can cause the height of the wedge to vary as much as $\frac{1}{4}$ in.

1. Check the fit of the mortises and tenons and make any adjustments necessary.
2. Assemble the case with just the top and bottom two shelves and clamp it tightly together.
3. Precisely mark the parts of the tenons that protrude past the sides. From these marks, lay out the mortises in the tenons that will accept the wedges.
4. Lay out the mortises as wide as the wedges and $\frac{3}{4}$ in. deep. Though the wedges are only $\frac{9}{16}$ in. thick where they sit tight in the mortises, you don't want them to bottom out in their holes before they pull the shelf up tight.

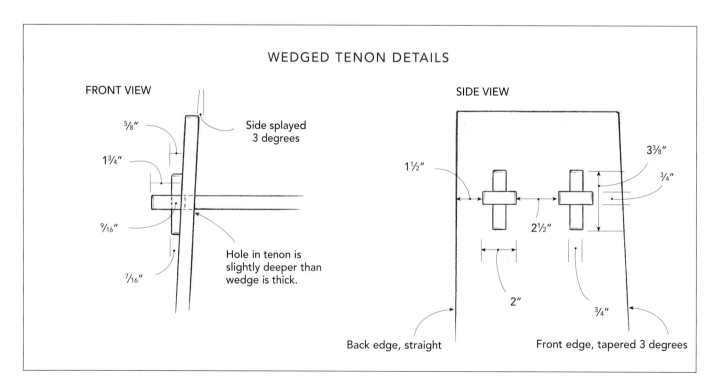

WEDGED TENON DETAILS

FRONT VIEW

$\frac{5}{8}$"

Side splayed 3 degrees

$1\frac{3}{4}$"

$\frac{9}{16}$"

$\frac{7}{16}$"

Hole in tenon is slightly deeper than wedge is thick.

SIDE VIEW

$1\frac{1}{2}$"

$3\frac{3}{8}$"

$\frac{3}{4}$"

$2\frac{1}{2}$"

2"

$\frac{3}{4}$"

Back edge, straight

Front edge, tapered 3 degrees

5. Working on the top of the shelves, measure out 9/16 in. from the marks on the tenons, draw a line, then measure back 3/4 in. and draw another line.

6. Measure out from the center of these lines 3/8 in. in each direction and connect your marks. This gives you a 3/4-in. by 3/4-in. hole for each wedge (see "Wedged Tenon Details").

7. Clamp a waste board under each tenon to prevent tearout on the opposite face when you cut the mortises.

8. Cut the mortises at 90 degrees using a 3/8-in. bit in a hollow-chisel mortiser. Nibble away at the edges of the holes until you reach the lines (see **photo I**). A mallet and chisel will do the work as well, though more slowly.

9. When you're finished cutting all the holes, clean them up with a small file.

Making and seating the wedges

Make the wedges only after the mortises are cut. It's far easier to adjust the wedge to fit the mortise than the other way around.

1. Rip and plane some 3/4-in.-square strips of zebrawood and cut them into 3 3/8-in. lengths (make sure you cut a few extra).

2. Make a small, simple carrier jig to hold the wedges when you cut the tapers on the bandsaw (see "Bandsaw Jig for Tapering the Wedges"). This jig ensures that all the wedges are exactly the same size so they fit into their holes in the same way.

3. Cut the tapers with the jig on the bandsaw.

4. Sand the cut edges of the wedges with a piece of sandpaper stuck to a flat block of wood to fine-tune the fit (see **photo J**). If everything prior to this has been done with care, there will be only minor adjustments.

5. Label the wedges so you can return them to their respective tenons later.

Fitting the middle shelves and cutting the biscuit slots

The four center shelves are attached to the sides with loose (unglued) biscuits. These aren't the easiest biscuit joints to cut because of the 3-degree angle of the sides.

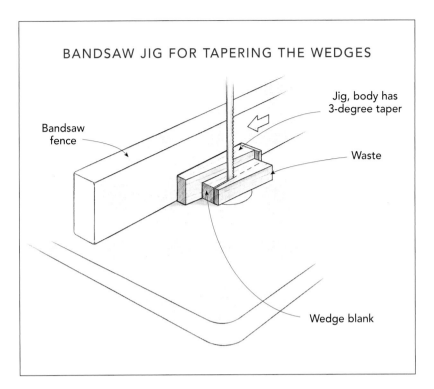

BANDSAW JIG FOR TAPERING THE WEDGES

Bandsaw fence

Jig, body has 3-degree taper

Waste

Wedge blank

Photo J: Sand the tapered faces of the wedges until they all sit at the same height.

BISCUIT SLOT CUTS FOR MIDDLE SHELVES

CUTTING SLOTS IN THE SHELF ENDS

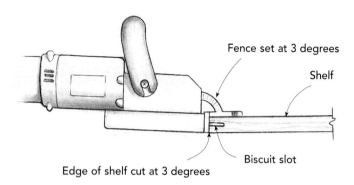

Fence set at 3 degrees

Shelf

Biscuit slot

Edge of shelf cut at 3 degrees

CUTTING SLOTS IN THE FACES OF THE SIDES

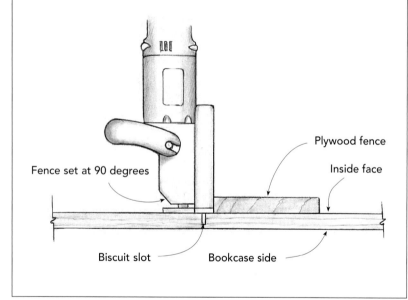

Plywood fence

Inside face

Fence set at 90 degrees

Biscuit slot

Bookcase side

HOW FAR SHOULD A WEDGE WEDGE?

The wedges on my bookcase drop farther down into their tenons than do the ones on David Fay's case. I made my wedges a little smaller so they'd go deeper, with the idea that they'd seat better. And since this piece can come apart, I thought this was important. I'm not sure if it makes any difference, but it seemed to me that it would. On the downside, I think the higher wedges look a little bit better. So there you go: Life is full of uncertainty and compromise.

1. Assemble the case, install the wedges, and make sure everything is tight.
2. Measure up from the bottom shelf, marking the location of the top of each shelf on both sides of the case.
3. Measure horizontally across the bookcase face with a straightedge and connect these marks. This gives you the width of each shelf (on the top face).
4. Starting with shelf blanks slightly over-sized in width and length, crosscut one edge of each on your table saw using the miter gauge set at 90 degrees and the blade tilted to 3 degrees.
5. Creep up on the finished width bit by bit, checking the fit on the case after each cut. Each shelf should fit tight but not bulge the sides or affect the fit of the other shelves.
6. Rip the front edges of the shelves at 3 degrees as well, sizing them 1/8 in. narrower than the depth of the case at each shelf location. When installed, the shelves will sit flush with the back and be recessed 1/8 in. from the front of the case.

7. Cut biscuit slots in the edges of the shelves, two to an edge. Reference these slots from the top of the shelves with the fence of your biscuit joiner set at 3 degrees (see "Biscuit Slot Cuts for Middle Shelves").

8. Knock down the bookcase before you cut the biscuit slots in the sides.

9. Draw layout lines across the sides at 90 degrees to the back, starting from the marks that indicate where the tops of the shelves intersect the sides.

10. Lay a piece of plywood along these lines to act as a fence for the biscuit joiner.

11. Cut the biscuit slots in the sides, positioning the joiner against the fence and plunging it in at 90 degrees to the side.

FINISHING AND FINAL ASSEMBLY

Rounding the edges

1. When you complete all the parts, do a final check for fit, fuss with anything that may still be bugging you, and disassemble the bookcase.

2. Work all the edges of the mortises and the holes for the wedges with a file to make the piece look soft and rounded. Round them until they have about a ⅛-in. radius on their edges.

3. Slightly round all the edges of the tenons, wedges, shelves, and sides with sandpaper to the same ⅛-in. radius.

4. Sand everything to 180 grit.

Applying the finish

At David Fay's suggestion I finished the piece with several coats of Formby's low-gloss tung oil. I felt an oil finish was important for a knockdown piece. Frequent assembly and disassembly would easily damage a harder, lacquered finish, and the wedges would, in all likelihood, scratch the finish around them when taken in and out. Oil finishes wear in

Photo K: The entire bookcase knocks down into a small pile of flat, small pieces—very handy for transportation.

these ways much better than lacquer finishes and are easily repaired when they dry out or become worn.

With this bookcase, final assembly is, frankly, optional. As a knockdown bookcase, it goes together and comes apart easily. And after you test-fit everything and finish all the pieces, the first thing you may want to do is knock it down to take it somewhere (see **photo K**).

SHAKER-STYLE BOOKCASE WITH DOORS

When I first saw the original of this case, I fell in love with its size and clean style. I'm a big fan of small-scale pieces, and this one, originally designed to fit beneath a windowsill, certainly qualifies. It's deceptively simple looking, but there is a fair amount of skill involved in building it. There are reasonably involved joints to cut, and the design doesn't allow you to hide mistakes. It's appearance relies in no small part on the exposed portions of its joinery.

The design comes from Christian Becksvoort, a furniture maker in New Gloucester, Maine, who makes furniture for the last active Shaker community at Sabbathday Lake. He is a long-time contributing editor to *Fine Woodworking* magazine and also the author of *The Shaker Legacy* (The Taunton Press, 1998).

With the exception of the dovetails joining the case, I used power tools to build this piece, but it struck me several times during construction that it would be a great piece to practice hand joinery on. Its small size also makes it very easy to handle during building.

This is also the first closed case in this book. Some might argue that it is more of a cabinet or a display case than a bookcase, but closed bookcases used to be quite common. In times when books were more rare and precious, it made sense to protect them behind doors, preferably ones that locked.

Shaker-Style Bookcase with Doors

BACK FRAME

THIS BOOKCASE IS COMPOSED of two sides dovetailed to a top and three shelves connected to the sides with sliding dovetails. A frame and two panels are set into a rabbet around the edge of the case's back. The front is completed with glass doors. A molding around the top is attached with dovetailed keys.

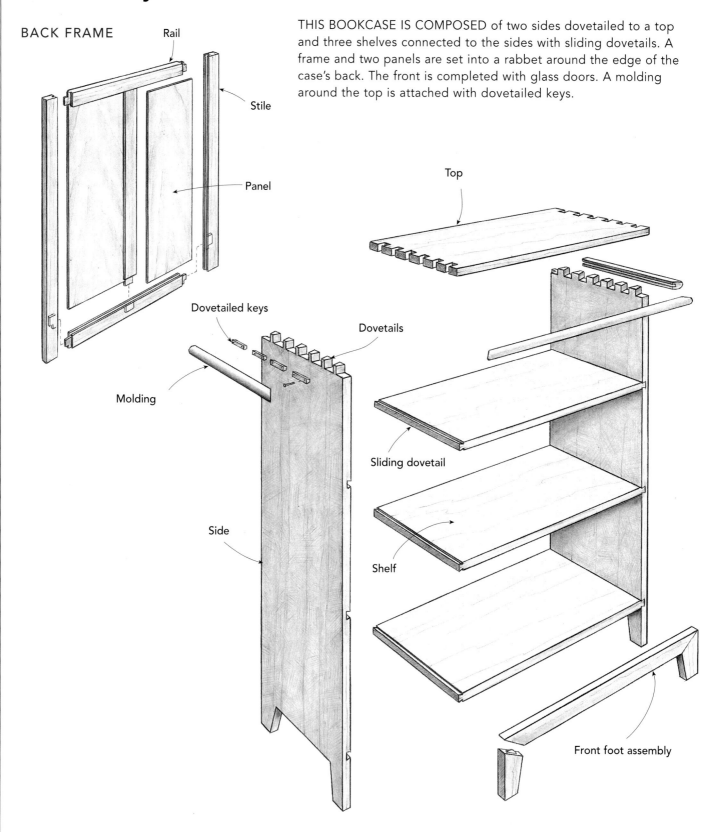

Rail

Stile

Panel

Top

Dovetailed keys

Dovetails

Molding

Side

Sliding dovetail

Shelf

Front foot assembly

FRONT VIEW

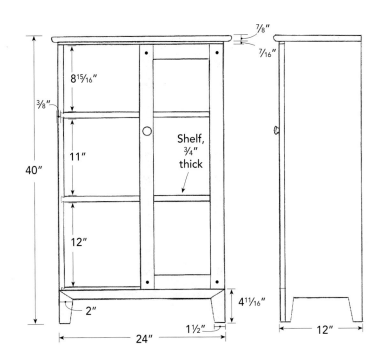

7/8"
7/16"
8 15/16"
3/8"
11"
40"
12"
Shelf, 3/4" thick
2"
24"
1 1/2"
4 11/16"

SIDE VIEW

12"

BACK FRAME

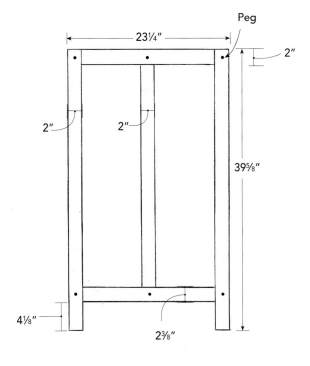

Peg
23 1/4"
2"
2"
2"
39 5/8"
4 1/8"
2 3/8"

DOOR FRAME

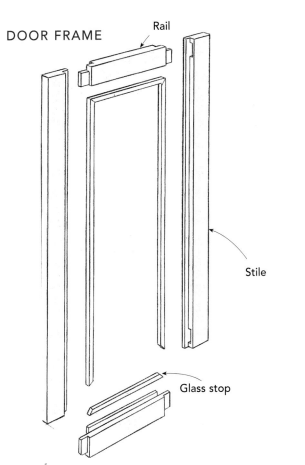

Rail

Stile

Glass stop

DOOR FRAME

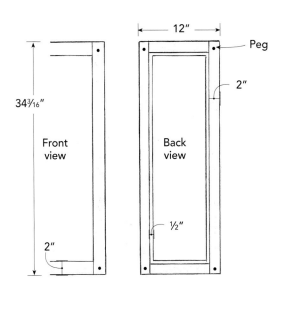

12"
Peg
2"
34 3/16"
Front view
Back view
1/2"
2"

BUILDING THE BOOKCASE STEP-BY-STEP

CUT LIST FOR SHAKER-STYLE BOOKCASE WITH DOORS

Carcase

2	Sides	40 in. x 11¼ in. x ¾ in.
1	Top	24 in. x 12 in. x ¾ in.
3	Shelves	23¼ in. x 10½ in. x ¾ in.
1	Foot kick	24 in. x 1¼ in. x ¾ in.
2	Feet	4½ in. x 2 in. x ¾ in.
1	Trim strip above doors	24 in. x ⁷⁄₁₆ in. x ¾ in.
1	Thumbnail molding	25¾ in. x ⅞ in. x ⅞ in.
2	Thumbnail molding	12⅞ in. x ⅞ in. x ⅞ in.

Doors

4	Door stiles	34³⁄₁₆ in. x 2 in. x ¾ in.
4	Door rails	11 in. x 2 in. x ¾ in.
4	Horizontal doorstops (molding)	9 in. x ⅜ in. x ⅜ in.
4	Vertical doorstops (molding)	31³⁄₁₆ in. x ⅜ in. x ⅜ in.
2	Glass for doors	31⅛ in. x 8¹⁵⁄₁₆ in., single strength

Back

2	Side stiles	39⅝ in. x 2 in. x ¾ in.
1	Center stile	34⅛ in. x 2 in. x ¾ in.
1	Top rail	22¼ in. x 2 in. x ¾ in.
1	Bottom rail	22¼ in. x 2⅜ in. x ¾ in.
2	Panels	32⅛ in. x 9⅝ in. x ¼ in.

Hardware

4	Hinges	1½ in. x 2 in. x ⅛ in.
2	Magnetic catches	⁷⁄₁₆ in. dia.

All parts are milled from solid cherry.

THERE IS A LOT OF DETAIL in this project, and it might seem intimidating at first. Taken a step at a time, no one part is too hard. I often build extremely large and complex projects, and I've found that while you can't lose sight of the whole, you can't let yourself be overwhelmed by all the work ahead. If you break the project down into manageable parts and take care of them one at a time, before you know it, it all comes together.

Start with the main carcase because, well, it's the main carcase and everything else is sized from and attached to this case. The other parts are really additions to the carcase.

MAKING THE CASE

Dovetailing the sides to the top

1. Size the stock for the sides, top, and shelves.

2. Cut a ½-in.-wide by ¾-in.-deep rabbet for the back panel in the inside edge of the top and sides on the table saw with a dado blade.

3. Lay out the dovetails that join the top to the sides. The tails should be cut on the top and the pins on the sides. This is because there will be more internal stress to push the sides apart than there will be to push the top off.

4. Cut the dovetails by hand or with a router and jig capable of through dovetails. I cut them by hand, tails first, since that is how Becksvoort cuts his.

5. The top overhangs the sides by ¾ in. at the front of the case, so lay out the front tail ¾ in. back from the edge.

6. Cut and pare the tails (see **photo A**).

7. Mark the pins on the top of the sides by positioning the top at 90 degrees to the side exactly above where it will be when assembled. Scribe the locations of the pins with a sharp knife (see **photo B**).

Photo A: Saw, then pare the tails with a chisel until you're satisfied they're right on. You'll use them to mark out the exact locations of the pins on the sides.

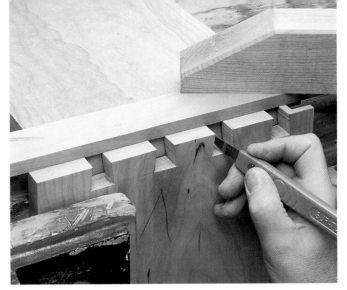

Photo B: Align the top and side the way they will go together and use the cut tails to mark the pin locations. A sharp knife with a point will give you great accuracy.

Photo C: Saw the sides of the pins with a fine-toothed backsaw slightly away from the line. A Japanese or Western backsaw will do the job well.

Photo D: You should be able to push or lightly tap a dovetail joint together. Any tighter and it will bind when glue is applied.

8. Saw the pins just inside the layout lines on the waste side (see **photo C**).

9. Cut out the waste with a coping saw and chisel.

10. Pare the sides of the pins to the lines with a chisel.

11. The pins and tails should be snug but not too tight. You should be able to dry-fit them without the aid of hammers and force. Remember that there is always some swelling once glue is applied (see **photo D**).

Photos E and F: To cut the legs on the sides, first cut to the line along both leg sides. Then cut up through the waste at an angle to the inside line (shown at left). This will give you access to cut flush along the line on the inside (shown at right). Register the feet against the bandsaw fence to cut a straight line.

Tip: Always clamp a piece of scrap where the router bit will exit the work-piece so it doesn't tear out the grain and leave a mess.

Cutting the foot profiles in the sides

1. Cut the foot profiles in the sides using a bandsaw fitted with a ¼-in. six-tooth-per-inch blade (see **photos E** and **F**). This size blade is my everyday blade. I use it for the majority of my bandsaw work, except resawing and tight scrollwork, and I've become very comfortable working with it. However, use whatever blade suits you best.

2. Clean up the cut with a sanding block.

Routing the dovetail slots in the sides

To cut the sliding dovetail slots in the sides for the three fixed shelves, I use a guide rail fixture and router. However, you don't need a guide rail fixture. A board can serve as a fence for the router, and a dovetail plane is the way to do it by hand.

1. Fit your router with an 8-degree, ½-in.-wide dovetail bit and set it to a depth of ⅜ in. (or half the thickness of the sides) (see **photos G** and **H**).

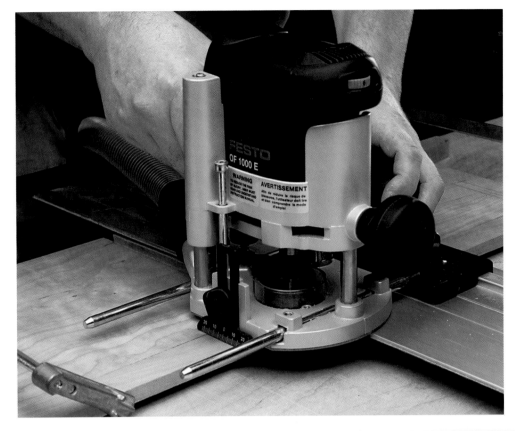

Photo G: Routing the dovetail slots is simple with a guide rail fixture. This Festo guide rail clamps to the board at 90 degrees and guides the router through the cut. With a piece of scrap clamped at the end, the bit won't splinter the grain where it shows.

2. Set the guide rail across the inside face of the sides. The edge of the guide registers where the top of the shelf will end up, making it easy to mark out and cut these slots.
3. Rout the slot slowly, but without burning the bit.

Routing the tails on the ends of the shelves

1. Set the same router bit you used to cut the dovetail slots in your router table to the same depth (⅜ in.).
2. Attach a tall board to the router-table fence as an extra support for the workpiece.
3. Carefully push this board onto the spinning bit before attaching it to the fence. This way, there is no large hole around the bit and the workpiece is fully supported in the cut.
4. Use the offcuts from crosscutting the shelves to make test cuts.

Photo H: The guide rail guides the router accurately through the cut by means of a stop that attaches to the router and precisely fits the guide rail.

Photo I: A tall fence on the router table guides the shelves when cutting the dovetails on the ends.

Photo J: Apply glue to the shelf dovetails only after they're most of the way into their slots. Also, spread some glue in the slots at the back of the shelves.

Tip: Since you are cutting the dovetails from both sides, any adjustment to the router fence is doubled in the cut.

5. Slowly creep up on the right fit with the test pieces, moving the fence in very small increments until you get it spot on. The perfect fit is not so tight that the shelf has to be hammered in but is snug when home.
6. Rout the dovetails on both ends of all three shelves. Make sure to keep them tight against the fence in the cut (see **photo I**).

Gluing up the carcase

1. Sand all the inside parts while the carcase is still apart.
2. Test-fit the carcase. If everything fits well, glue and clamp the dovetailed sides and top together, taking care to keep these three pieces square.
3. Once the glue is dry, fit the shelves one by one. Slide each shelf into its slot from the front without glue, stopping when approximately 3 in. is still exposed.
4. At that point, apply glue to the exposed ends of the dovetails and in the slots at the back of the shelves (see **photo J**).
5. Tap the shelves home until their fronts are flush with the front of the sides, and clamp each shelf across the case at the front and back just for insurance.
6. The case sides extend below the bottom shelf, but not by much, and only a small portion of the front and back of the shelf is glued. To give the carcase some extra strength, add two small blocks, glued and screwed at each end of the underside of the bottom shelf (visible in **photo K**).

ADDING THE CARCASE DETAILS

Front foot assembly

The front foot assembly consists of a horizontal member and two feet connected with asymmetrical miters (see "Mitered Base Assembly").

1. Mill a single piece ¾ in. thick, 2 in. wide, and 34 in. long.
2. Cut a 5-in.-long piece off each end and rip the remaining piece to 1¼ in.
3. Lay out the miters by simply putting the parts on top of one another and marking the edges of their intersection. Then connect the corners and you've got your layout lines (see "Laying Out the Asymmetrical Miters").
4. Cut the miters on the bandsaw and sand them perfectly flat.
5. Use a #0 biscuit to give the end-grain miter some strength. Center the biscuit so it doesn't shouldn't show at the top or bottom of the joint.

6. Glue up the foot assembly with clamps, clamping across the miters both side to side and top to bottom.

7. To even out the length of the feet, run the whole assembly over the table saw with the horizontal member registering against the fence. This way you can crosscut both legs to exactly 4½ in. long.

8. Cut the tapers on the inside edges of the feet on a bandsaw. Sand the edges smooth.

9. Glue the assembly onto the case (see **photo K**).

10. To ensure that the feet won't come off in the near or distant future, add glue blocks on the inside corners where the sides meet the front and the back.

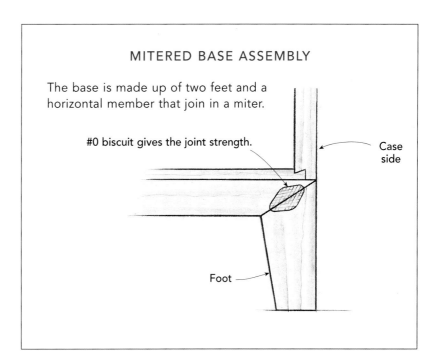

MITERED BASE ASSEMBLY

The base is made up of two feet and a horizontal member that join in a miter.

#0 biscuit gives the joint strength.

Case side

Foot

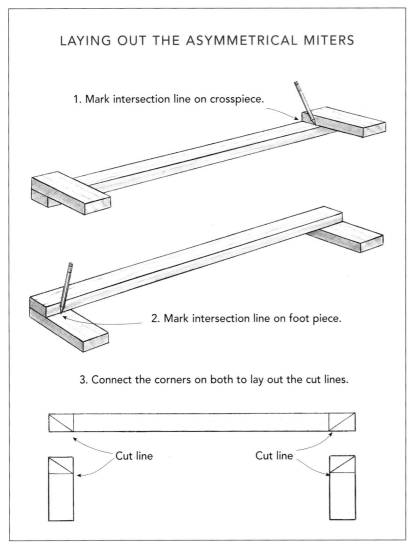

LAYING OUT THE ASYMMETRICAL MITERS

1. Mark intersection line on crosspiece.

2. Mark intersection line on foot piece.

3. Connect the corners on both to lay out the cut lines.

Cut line

Cut line

Photo K: A little glue is enough to attach the front foot assembly to the carcase.

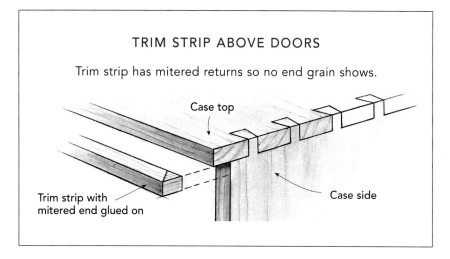

TRIM STRIP ABOVE DOORS

Trim strip has mitered returns so no end grain shows.

Case top

Trim strip with
mitered end glued on

Case side

*Tip: Don't let the
molding wander in
the cut because the
bit is trapped. If the
molding moves
away from the
fence, the bit will
cut off course. Use
a profiled feather-
board to keep the
molding on track.*

Trim strip

1. Mill a ⁷⁄₁₆-in. by ³⁄₄-in. decorative trim strip.
2. To avoid end grain showing on this strip, miter the ends and add little triangular blocks, securing them with cyanoacrylate glue, like Hot Stuff Super T CA (see Sources on pp. 182-183). It's a fragile joint, but this piece will be glued to the underside of the top, so not much can happen to it.
3. Attach the strip just above the doors and below the top (see "Trim Strip above Doors").

THE THUMBNAIL MOLDING

Making the molding

The thumbnail molding around the top of the case has an asymmetrical profile. I couldn't buy any molding that matched this profile, and I didn't have a cutter or combination of cutters that came close. So I made it myself, which is not that difficult (for the profile, see "Detail of Thumbnail Molding").

1. Scribe the profile on the end of a board several inches wide and the same thickness as the molding.
2. Cut away the majority of the waste on the table saw.
3. Taking long, even strokes with a hand-plane, shave the board edge into the profile.
4. Sand the edge smooth.
5. Rip the finished molding off the edge of the board, and cut it to the lengths you need.

Attaching the front piece of molding

1. Miter one end of the front molding, position it, and mark the other end.
2. Cut the second miter and glue the molding to the front of the case. The grain direction of the molding is the same as the case, so wood movement isn't a problem.

Routing the dovetailed slot

To attach the molding to the sides, I used Chris Becksvoort's dovetail key system (see "Cross-Grain Molding Attachment").

1. Remove the bulk of the dovetailed slot in the two pieces of side molding with a straight bit on a router table.
2. Using a ¹⁄₂-in.-wide dovetail bit set to a depth of about ¹⁄₄ in., rout the finished dovetail slot (see **photo L**).

Making the dovetailed key

1. Mill a blank that's a little thicker than ¹⁄₂ in., about 3 in. wide, and a few inches longer than the case sides.
2. Use a piece of scrap of the same thickness to make a test piece, adjusting the fence on the router table until the fit is snug but not binding.
3. Rout a dovetailed profile onto both sides of the blank, top, and bottom (see **photo M**).
4. Saw off the keys on the table saw with a little to spare.
5. Mill the keys to final thickness in a planer, taking material off the narrower side of the keys until they are just a tad shallower than the slots in the molding. This slight difference will help pull the molding tight to the case.

Attaching the keys as continuous strips

One long key screwed to the sides wouldn't work because it wouldn't allow the sides to move back and forth freely. I install the keys on the sides as one long strip, and chop out sections to make a series of keys. It's simply much easier than trying to attach separate keys and fussing with them to make sure they're all in line.

CROSS-GRAIN MOLDING ATTACHMENT

Attaching molding to a solid carcase side has always been a problem because its grain runs perpendicular to the grain of the sides. Molding that's glued fast or nailed to the case sides will eventually fail. It will either cause the case sides to crack by preventing them from moving, or the molding will pop off when the side moves. On many antique pieces, the solution to this problem was simple: nail the molding in place and whatever happens, happens!

Chris Becksvoort uses a technique that solves this problem. While the front molding is simply glued in place, the side molding slides on dovetail keys. These hold the molding snug to the sides without restricting seasonal movement. The molding will last as long as the case piece, and the case sides will not crack. The only downside is that it's not as simple as nailing on molding with a few brads.

DETAIL OF THUMBNAIL MOLDING

On the carcase sides, dovetailed keys, spot-glued and screwed to the carcase, secure the molding without restraining movement.

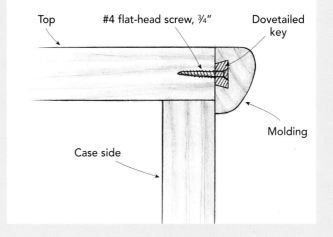

Top — #4 flat-head screw, ¾" — Dovetailed key — Molding — Case side

Photo L: Rout the dovetail slots in the molding on the router table. Use an angled featherboard to keep the molding against the fence. Apply solid downward pressure when routing the slots. Any unwanted movement of molding will ruin the slots.

Photo M: To make the dovetailed keys, first make some test pieces and fit them to the molding. Then run the key stock through on both sides.

Photo O: The thumbnail molding shouldn't slide on too easily but shouldn't need to be hammered into place.

Photo N: Chop out the waste between the keys, don't saw it. A saw might cut into the face or edge of the carcase.

1. Hold a strip of molding against the side of the case, with the top edge of the molding flush with or just slightly proud of the top of the case (you can sand this flush later).

2. With a knife, mark both the top and bottom of the dovetailed slot at the front and rear of the case.

3. Connect these marks using a straightedge to find the proper location of the key strip.

4. Lay out what part of the keys will be kept and what will be waste. Mark out the center of the key strip, and then divide each half into three keys separated by ½-in. spaces. Mark for screws about ½ in. to each side of the centers of the individual keys.

5. Put a dab of glue at the center of each of the marked keys,

6. Temporarily attach the strip with some ¾-in., #20 brads.

7. Drill and countersink holes for the ¾-in., #4 screws that will hold the keys in place. Drive the screws in and attach the keys.

8. Chop out the waste between the keys with a chisel and hammer (see **photo N**).

Sliding on the molding

1. Test the fit of the molding. It should slide onto the keys without binding (see **photo O**). If the fit is too tight, a little light sanding of the tops of the keys may be necessary.

2. Miter the front ends of the molding.

3. Put a dab of glue on the miter and on the first 2 in. of the case, and tap the molding home.

4. Clamp the molding across the case at the miter.

5. After the glue has dried, saw off the excess at the back of the case.

MAKING THE DOORS AND BACK PANEL

Milling the parts for the doors and back panel

The doors and back panel are similar in size and construction, though the back holds panels and the doors hold glass panes. Nevertheless, it makes sense to mill most of the parts at the same time. The rails and stiles are all the same thickness and width, ¾ in. by 2 in. I used quartersawn stock for the frames to minimize wood movement.

Making the backs

The back is a mortise-and-tenoned frame with floating panels (see "Back Frame Joinery").

Back Frame Joinery

Groove the stiles and rails first. Then cut the mortises in the stiles and rails.
There are three different mortise locations, but all are the same size.

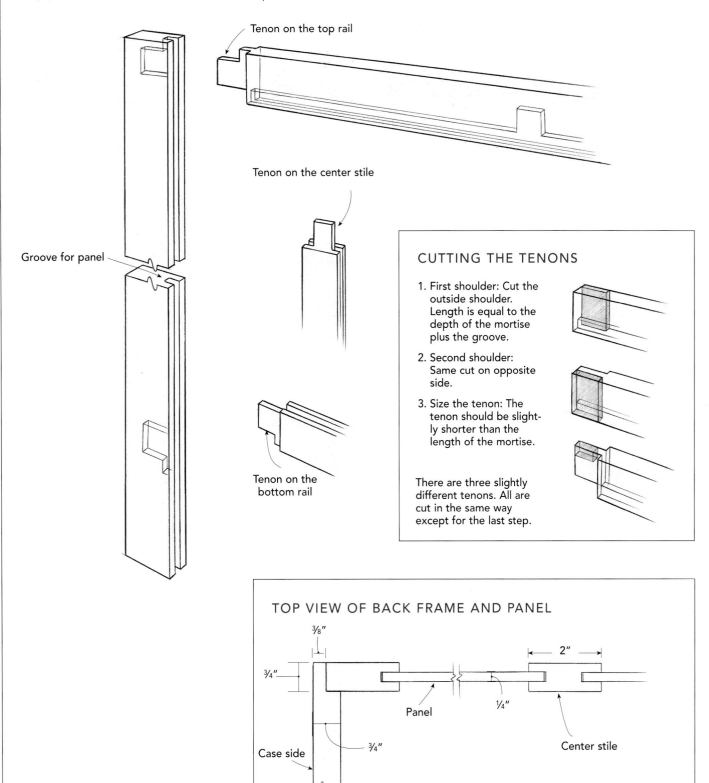

Tenon on the top rail

Tenon on the center stile

Groove for panel

Tenon on the bottom rail

CUTTING THE TENONS

1. First shoulder: Cut the outside shoulder. Length is equal to the depth of the mortise plus the groove.

2. Second shoulder: Same cut on opposite side.

3. Size the tenon: The tenon should be slightly shorter than the length of the mortise.

There are three slightly different tenons. All are cut in the same way except for the last step.

TOP VIEW OF BACK FRAME AND PANEL

⅜"

¾"

¾"

Case side

Panel

¼"

2"

Center stile

3. Cut the cheeks of the tenons on the table saw with a tenoning jig, or however you prefer.

4. Cut the shoulders of the tenons on the table saw with a miter gauge.

5. Try to cut the two 1/4-in.-thick panels for the back from one resawn 4/4 board. They are less than 10 in. wide, and so should fit most bandsaws and planers. This allows you to book-match the panels so one looks like the mirror image of the other.

6. Sand the panels to 180 grit.

7. Glue and clamp the frames together, making sure they are square.

8. When the glue dries, pin the joints with 1/4-in.-diameter, 7/8-in.-long sections of cherry dowel. Drive the pins all the way through the joints. The tenons are quite small, so one pin per joint is sufficient.

9. Sand the inside of the frames.

10. Fit the back to the carcase. Using a block plane, shave small amounts off each edge of the back until it fits the rabbet just so.

11. Mark the location of the shelves on the back of the frame and glue the back into the rabbet.

12. After the glue dries, drill holes and countersink for trim-head finishing screws, one at the center of each shelf and one near each end.

13. Fill the screw holes with small cherry pegs, then sand the outside of the back and ease all the edges.

Making the doors

The construction of the doors is similar to the back, though with a few differences. The doors have rabbets instead of grooves because the glass panes shouldn't be locked into place. The rail tenons for the doors are a bit different from the tenons in the back because they have offset shoulders to fit this rabbet (see "Door Frame Joinery").

1. Rabbet the door frame pieces with a dado blade on the table saw.

Photo P: The mortises in the rails of the back frame are easily cut on a hollow-chisel mortiser.

Tip: Purposely build the back a tiny bit (1/16 in.+) oversize so that you can fit it perfectly to the carcase without gaps.

1. Run a 1/4-in. groove down the center of the inside edge of each of the outside frame pieces and along both edges of the center stile.

2. Cut 1/4-in. mortises inside the groove toward the end of each stile and in the center of the top and bottom rails using a hollow-chisel mortiser (see **photo P**).

Door Frame Joinery

Rabbet the stiles and rails first. Then cut the mortises in the stiles.

Door stile

CUTTING THE OFFSET TENONS IN THE RAILS

1. First shoulder: Cut outside shoulder of tenon. Length is equal to the depth of the mortise plus the rabbet.

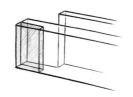

2. Second shoulder: The inside shoulder of the tenon is shorter to compensate for the rabbet in the stile.

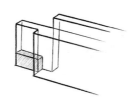

3. Size the tenon: The tenon should be slightly shorter than the length of the mortise.

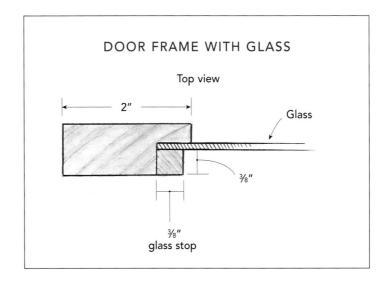

DOOR FRAME WITH GLASS

Top view

2"

Glass

⅜"

⅜"
glass stop

Fitting the doors to the case

The doors fit all the way to the outside edges of the case and top to bottom between the top trim strip and the top of the foot assembly. Fitting them into this space to create a smooth flush front is not a big deal.

1. Working from the actual size of the finished case, lightly trim each door on a jointer, taking equal amounts off the top and bottom edges until you have a 3/32-in. gap at the top and bottom.
2. Trim the inside edges of both doors until you have the same 3/32-in. gap between the doors. Because I used quartersawn stock, total movement for both doors, side to side, should be less than 1/16 in.

Hanging the doors

I hung the doors with 1½-in. by 2-in. by ⅛-in. polished drawn brass flat-back butt hinges from Whitechapel Ltd. (hinge #107H5P; see Sources on pp. 182-183).

1. Lay out mortises for the hinges in the doors, first scribing around them with a knife, then routing out most of the waste.
2. Clean up the corners and edges with a chisel, and screw the hinges in the doors temporarily with one screw each.
3. Mark the positions of the hinge mortises on the edges of the case sides by laying a door on the case, making sure the outside edge is flush and the door is centered top to bottom.
4. Mark the location of the hinge at the butt.
5. Remove the hinges from the doors and position them between the marks, with the barrel of the hinge acting as a depth stop. This way you can mark out the perimeter of the hinges in the right place.
6. Rout the mortise and pare it square as on the doors (see **photo R**).

Adding the knobs and glass

1. Either turn some knobs on a lathe or buy them from a woodworking-supply store.
2. Drill holes for the knobs.

Photo Q: The door frame mortises on the four stiles are cut using a hollow-chisel mortiser.

Tip: When you joint the doors, make sure you keep them square.

2. Cut the mortises in the four stiles using a hollow-chisel mortiser (see **photo Q**), and cut the tenons in the same way as you did for the back.
3. Glue up the doors, following the same pattern as for the back.
4. At this point also rip, plane, and sand eight ⅜-in.-square pieces of stock for the glass stops.

Photo R: Rout the hinge mortises in the side of the case, and square them up with a chisel.

3. Dab a little glue in the holes and firmly press the knobs in place. If they are tight, you can use a clamp and a block of wood to seat them.

4. Drill holes in the upper shelf for round magnetic catches and recess the strikes into the backs of the door stiles. Other types of catches will also work fine.

5. Have some glass cut for the doors about $\frac{1}{16}$ in. smaller than the openings. I used regular window glass, which is about $\frac{3}{32}$ in. thick, but it might be nice to use art glass of some kind or a period-type glass.

FINISHING UP

Sanding and applying tung oil and glass stops

1. Sand the outside and front of the case, the back, and doors through 180 grit, easing all the edges.

2. Apply tung oil to the case. I used Sutherland Welles Polymerized Tung Oil, Medium Luster (see Sources on pp. 182-183)

to finish the case. I recommend this finish highly. It takes some getting used to, and it's a fair amount of work to apply correctly, but it's a wonderful, lustrous, long-lasting finish (follow the directions on the can). It's the closest thing to a lacquer finish you can get from an oil.

3. Glaze the doors and install the glass stops. Predrill and nail the stops in place with $\frac{3}{4}$-in.-long brass escutcheon pins, and then hang the doors.

4. Add small clear door bumpers (available from most woodworking suppliers) to the doorstops, top and bottom, so the doors close quietly. Mr. Becksvoort uses leather buttons, which I think is a nice touch.

Tip: Glass suppliers are notorious for cutting to the nearest $\frac{1}{2}$ in., so its best to take the doors and have the glass cut to fit.

Tip: There is no point in sanding past 180 grit, since the finishing process requires a lot of steel wool, oil, and elbow grease, which will make everything shine anyway.

ARTS AND CRAFTS BOOKCASE

Like much Arts and Crafts furniture, this bookcase announces the details of its construction, with wedged through mortise-and-tenon joints and a bright finish that helps the grain stand out. The original is called the Glasgow bookcase, which is part of a line of Arts and Crafts inspired furniture produced by Susan Mack and Kevin Rodel. They are the husband and wife team behind Mack & Rodel, Fine Furniture and Design Studio in Pownal, Maine.

The bookcase is described in their catalog as an earlier effort at an "original" design in the Arts and Crafts tradition. They blended influences from the work of many Scottish designers and artists, such as Charles Rennie Mackintosh, that collectively made up what was known as the Glasgow style.

Designed to fit in a fairly narrow space (it's only 36 in. wide), this bookcase is ideal for small rooms in bungalows, cottages, or apartments. The doors make it appropriate for books or materials that require care and protection but that you don't need constant access to nor want to put on display.

Most original Arts and Crafts pieces were built with white oak, then fumed dark with concentrated ammonia. I chose to build this piece with cherry because I liked the more contemporary look and was uncertain about working with ammonia.

Arts and Crafts Bookcase

THIS ARTS AND CRAFTS STYLE enclosed bookcase is built with frames and panels tenoned into the corner posts. The top and bottom are floating plywood panels. The door frames are mortised and tenoned and hold Reamy glass panes. The inlay on the posts and rear top rail is ebony, as are the wedges in the through tenons and the pegs over the screws on the bottom of the posts.

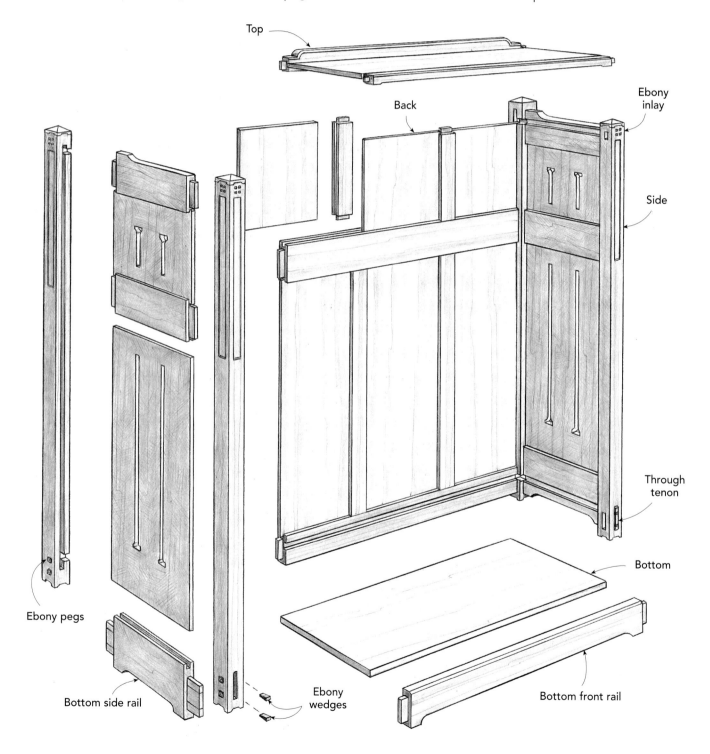

Top

Back

Ebony inlay

Side

Through tenon

Bottom

Ebony pegs

Bottom side rail

Ebony wedges

Bottom front rail

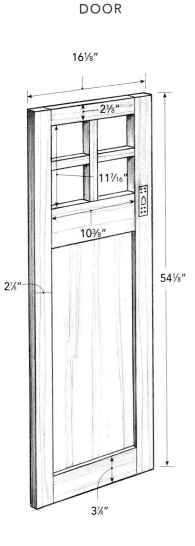

DOOR

16⅛″

2⅛″

11⁷⁄₁₆″

10⅜″

2⁷⁄₈″

54⅛″

3⅞″

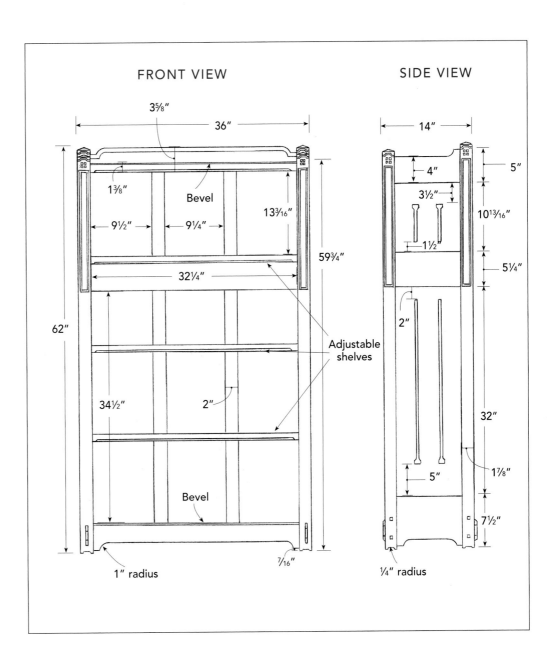

FRONT VIEW

SIDE VIEW

3⅝″

36″

1⅜″

Bevel

13³⁄₁₆″

9½″

9¼″

59¾″

32¼″

62″

Adjustable
shelves

34½″

2″

2″

Bevel

7⁄₁₆″

1″ radius

14″

4″

5″

3½″

10¹³⁄₁₆″

1½″

5¼″

2″

32″

1⁷⁄₈″

5″

7½″

¼″ radius

BUILDING THE BOOKCASE STEP-BY-STEP

THIS PIECE has to be put together and taken apart many times during construction because you need to check the fit of mortises and the orientation of parts before assembly. There is a lot to keep track of, and it can be a bit overwhelming. You'll sometimes feel as if you're not getting anywhere and are building a collection of parts.

To help keep things straight, after you mill the parts separate the whole into subsections

CUT LIST FOR ARTS AND CRAFTS BOOKCASE

Side Assemblies

2	Corner posts	1⅞ in. x 1⅞ in. x 62 in.
2	Corner posts	1⅞ in. x 1⅞ in. x 61 in.
2	Panels	11 in. x 10¹⁵⁄₁₆ in. x ⅜ in.
2	Panels	11 in. x 32¾ in. x ⅜ in.
2	Rails	5 in. x 11½ in. x 1 in.
2	Rails	5¼ in. x 11½ in. x 1 in.
2	Rails	7½ in. x 14¼ in. x 1 in.

Back Assembly

2	Panels	10¼ in. x 13¹⁵⁄₁₆ in. x ⅜ in.
1	Panel	10 in. x 13¹⁵⁄₁₆ in. x ⅜ in.
2	Panels	10¼ in. x 36¼ in. x ⅜ in.
1	Panel	10 in. x 36¼ in. x ⅜ in.
1	Rail	3⅝ in. x 33½ in. x 1 in.
1	Rail	5¼ in. x 33½ in. x 1 in.
1	Rail	4 in. x 33½ in. x 1 in.
2	Stiles	2 in. x 14⁷⁄₁₆ in. x 1 in.
2	Stiles	2 in. x 36¾ in. x 1 in.

Top Assembly

1	Top	12⅞ in. x 33¾ in. x ¾ in.
1	Front rail	1⅜ in. x 33½ in. x 1⅝ in.

Bottom Assembly

1	Bottom	12⅞ in. x 33¾ in. x ¾ in.
1	Front rail	4 in. x 33½ in. x 1⅝ in.

Shelves

2	Shelves	11 in. x 33½ in. x 1 in.
1	Shelf	11 in. x 32 in. x 1 in.
4	Shelf supports	32 in. x ¼ in. x 1 in.
4	Shelf supports	4 in. x ¼ in. x 1 in.
6	Shelf supports	9¼ in. x ¼ in. x 1 in.

Doors

1	Rail	13⅛ in. x 2⅛ in. x 1 in.
1	Rail	13⅛ in. x 5¼ in. x 1 in.
1	Rail	13⅛ in. x 3⅞ in. x 1 in.
2	Stiles	54⅛ in. x 2⅞ in. x 1 in.
2	Cross dividers	14³⁄₁₆ in. x 1 in. x 1 in.
2	Cross dividers	13⅛ in. x 1 in. x 1 in.
2	Doorstops	32¼ in. x ⅜ in. x ⅜ in.
8	Ebony wedges	⅛ in. x ⅜ in. x 1¼ in.
8	Ebony plugs	⅜ in. x ⅜ in. x 1 in.
24 squares	Ebony inlay	⁵⁄₁₆ in. x ⁵⁄₁₆ in. x 1¼ in.
20 linear ft.	Ebony inlay	⅛ in. x ¼ in.

Hardware

4	Straight knife hinges	½ in.
4	Bullet catches	⁷⁄₁₆ in. dia.
2	Arts and Crafts style pulls	

All parts are made of solid cherry except where otherwise indicated.

(sides, back, and so on) and focus on them one at a time. In the end, the bookcase will come together rather suddenly: One morning it will be a pile of pieces, and by evening it will all be clamped up.

MILLING AND SHAPING THE PARTS

Milling all the parts

Mill all the stock for the project at once because each section is interdependent. It would become very confusing to build one part or section without having the next on hand to relate measurements.

1. Glue up pieces for the top, bottom, and the three shelves from smaller pieces, unless you have some very wide lumber.

2. Make up a rough-size cut list according to the measurements provided.

3. Mill all stock for this project at one time. This includes the corner posts, all the rails, the stiles for the back, the top, bottom, shelves, the door stock, and the back and side panels.

Milling the side panels

The four side panels have long and thin openings in them. They look difficult to make, but in fact are quite easy because they're assembled (see "Book-Matching Side Panels with Cutout Detail"). The procedure is the same for both the short and the long panels.

1. Mill 8/4 stock square and parallel on all sides to 3⅞ in. wide and the approximate length of the panels.

2. Cut half of the profile on each edge of these blanks on the table saw using a miter gauge and a dado cutter. First crosscut a ½-in.-deep dado on both sides of all pieces with a ¼-in.-wide dado cutter, then nibble away the remainder with your widest dado cutter set to cut a depth of ¼ in.

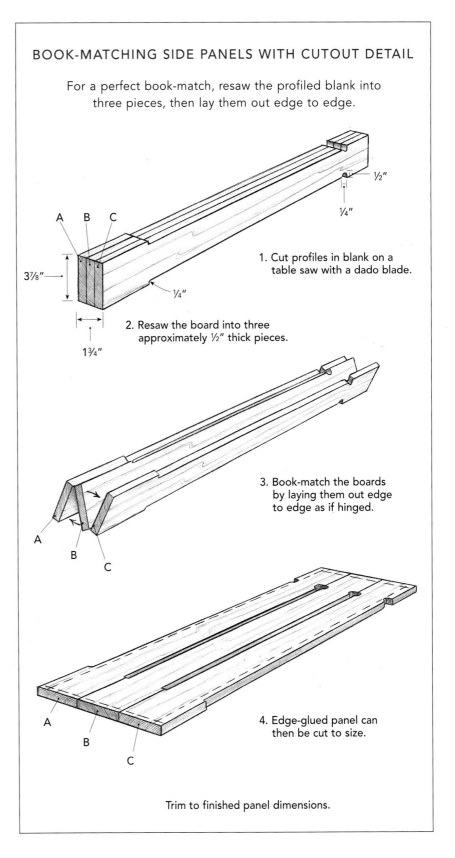

BOOK-MATCHING SIDE PANELS WITH CUTOUT DETAIL

For a perfect book-match, resaw the profiled blank into three pieces, then lay them out edge to edge.

1. Cut profiles in blank on a table saw with a dado blade.

2. Resaw the board into three approximately ½" thick pieces.

3. Book-match the boards by laying them out edge to edge as if hinged.

4. Edge-glued panel can then be cut to size.

Trim to finished panel dimensions.

MORTISE LAYOUT ON POSTS

Take all measurements from the bottom edge; the top mortises should be approximately 1" from the top of the posts. All mortises are centered on the posts, 3/8" wide and 5/8" deep, except the through mortises for the bottom side rails.

FRONT POST

Front corner post is 61" high.

1"

3"

Side faces

Front face

11¹³⁄₁₆"

4¼"

54⅝"

34¹⁄₁₆"

Through mortises

3"

4½"

¹⁵⁄₁₆"

¹⁵⁄₁₆"

REAR POST

Rear post is 62" high.

2"

4"

Back face

14¹⁄₁₆"

11¹³⁄₁₆"

4¼"

4¼"

34¹⁄₁₆"

36½"

4½"

3"

¹⁵⁄₁₆"

¹⁵⁄₁₆"

¹⁵⁄₁₆"

---

3. Cut and smooth the curve with a rasp, files, and finally sandpaper.

4. Resaw the blanks into three boards of the same thickness, a little more than ½ in. thick.

5. Book-match the boards and glue them together. This creates the openings.

6. Plane and sand to ⅜ in. thick. At this point the panels are still oversize. Determine the finished width and height once you have the corner posts and rails done.

Cutting joinery on the corner posts

The four corner posts are probably the most complicated parts in the bookcase. All panels and rails join into them.

1. Lay out the mortises in the corner posts (see "Mortise Layout on Posts").

2. Cut the mortises using a hollow-chisel mortiser (see **photo A**). A plunge router and jig or a chisel and hammer will also do the job well.

3. Mortise the back rails to accept the vertical stiles.

4. Rout ⅜-in.-wide stopped grooves for the side and back panels in the posts on a router table. Start and stop this groove in a mortise so you don't have to plunge the bit into the wood (see **photo B**).

Cutting details on the posts

The tops of the corner posts have a double bevel, creating a pyramid-like peak (see "Post Top Bevel Detail").

1. Cut a 45-degree bevel ¼ in. down from the top of each post on the table saw using a miter gauge set to 90 degrees (see **photo C** on p. 120).

2. Cut a second, 7-degree bevel ⅛ in. up from the first bevel cut, forming the peak.

> *Tip: Be careful not to cut a groove above the top mortises, below the bottom mortises, or on the inside face of the front post where the doors will attach. Clearly mark the faces to prevent these mistakes.*

Photo A: A hollow-chisel mortiser cuts square mortises in the posts quickly and efficiently.

Photo B: Cut the panel grooves in the posts on a router table. Start and stop the cuts from inside the mortises where the bit can't catch as you lower the post down or lift it off.

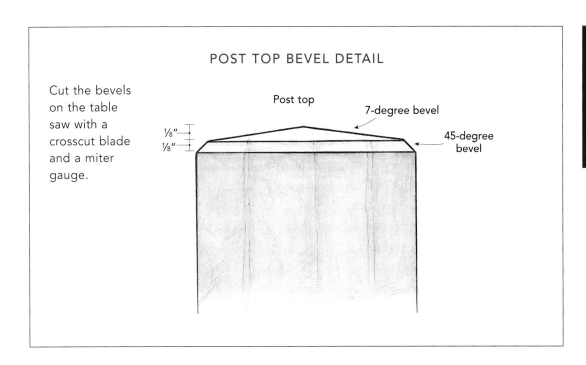

POST TOP BEVEL DETAIL

Cut the bevels on the table saw with a crosscut blade and a miter gauge.

Post top

7-degree bevel

45-degree bevel

⅛"
⅛"

Tip: To reference the bevels in the same place on each face, use a stop block at the far end of the miter gauge from the blade.

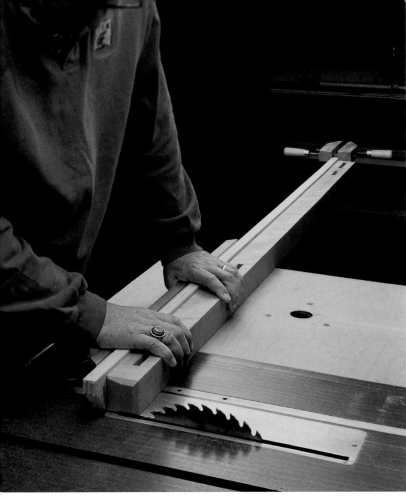

Photo C: Cut the two bevels on the top of the posts on the table saw with a miter gauge.

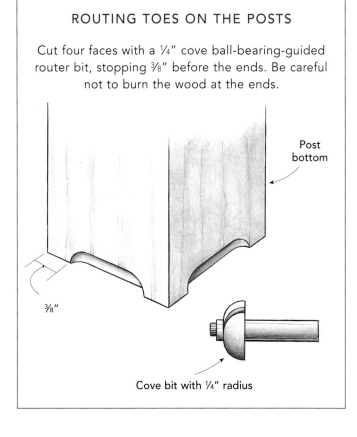

ROUTING TOES ON THE POSTS

Cut four faces with a ¼" cove ball-bearing-guided router bit, stopping ⅜" before the ends. Be careful not to burn the wood at the ends.

Post bottom

⅜"

Cove bit with ¼" radius

Tip: A short fence attached to the table-saw rip fence keeps the loose cut-offs from jamming between the saw-blade and the fence.

3. Cut coves on the bottom of all four sides of each post with a ¼-in. cove ball-bearing-guided router bit in a router table (see "Routing Toes on the Posts").

Cutting joinery on the rails and stiles

Tackle all of the tenons on the rails and stiles at once. All of them are blind mortise-and-tenon joints, with two exceptions: The bottom side rails are through-wedged mortises and tenons, and the bottom front and back rails are stub tenons screwed in place from the opposite side of the post.

1. Make the cheek cuts first on the bandsaw. Use a spacer block to keep the depth of cut even, and set the fence to give you tenons just a hair wider than ⅜ in. to allow precise fitting to the mortises later (see **photo D**).

2. Make the shoulder cuts on the table saw using a miter gauge and a short fence to register the distance from the end of the tenon to the shoulder (see **photo E**).

3. Bandsaw the slots in the through tenons that will accept the ebony wedges, making two overlapping cuts for a finished slot about 1½ times the width of the blade.

Joinery for the top and bottom assemblies

Dadoes in the side and back rails capture the top and bottom panels of this bookcase (see "Top and Bottom Assembly").

1. Cut ¾-in.-wide by 5/16-in.-deep dadoes in the side and back rails on a table saw fitted with a ¾-in.-wide dado blade.

2. Switch to a ⅜-in.-wide dado cutter and mill the ⅜-in.-wide by ⅜-in.-deep grooves in the rails and stiles that accept the side and back panels.

Photo D: Cut the tenon cheeks of the rails and stiles on the bandsaw. Clamp a block to the fence as a depth stop.

Photo E: Cut the tenon shoulders on the table saw for a clean edge.

Top and Bottom Assembly

The top and bottom assemblies are identical except for the front rails.

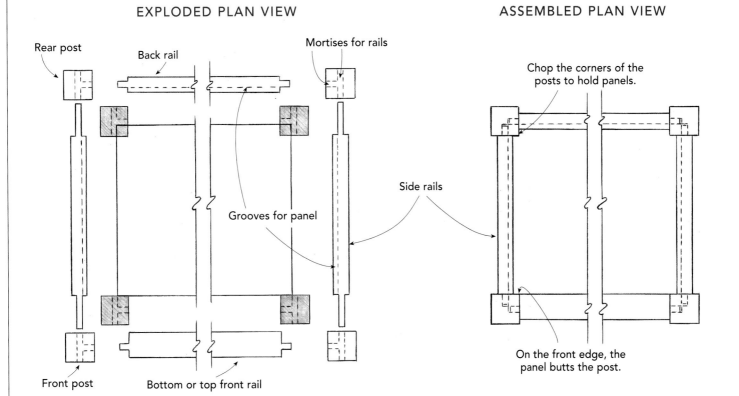

EXPLODED PLAN VIEW

Rear post

Back rail

Mortises for rails

Grooves for panel

Side rails

Front post

Bottom or top front rail

ASSEMBLED PLAN VIEW

Chop the corners of the posts to hold panels.

Side rails

On the front edge, the panel butts the post.

Photo F: A ¼-in.-wide blade on the bandsaw is thin enough to cut out the round corners of the rail details.

Shaping the rails

The top and bottom rails on the sides and the bottom front and top back rails have decorative cutouts.

1. Lay out these cutouts and bandsaw them close to the line (see **photo F**).
2. Smooth the cutouts with machine and hand sanding.
3. Cut a wide, shallow bevel on the top edges of the top and bottom front rails with a block plane.
4. Cut a cove on the underside of the top front rail with a ¼-in. piloted cove bit, stopping 1 in. from each end. The inside edge of this cove and the back of the bevel on the bottom rail line up with the front of the doors.

Attaching the top and bottom to their front rails

The top and bottom of the piece are captured, but not glued in dadoes in the side and back rails. This allows them to expand and contract

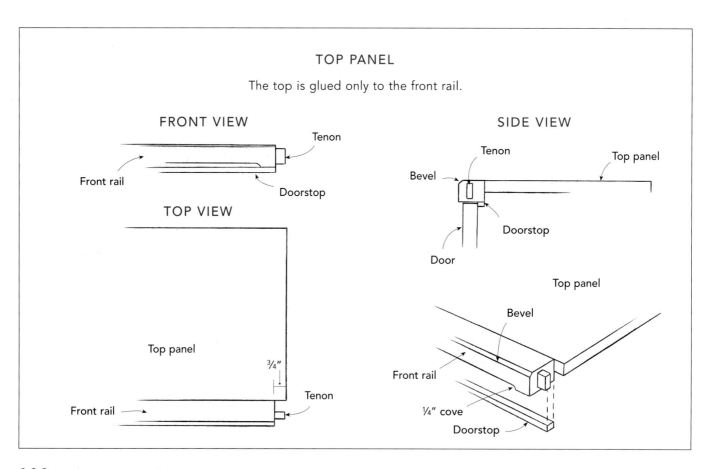

TOP PANEL

The top is glued only to the front rail.

FRONT VIEW

Tenon

Front rail

Doorstop

TOP VIEW

Top panel

¾"

Front rail

Tenon

SIDE VIEW

Tenon

Bevel

Top panel

Doorstop

Door

Top panel

Bevel

Front rail

¼" cove

Doorstop

without splitting the piece. Preassemble these now to make final glue-up easier.

1. Attach the top panel flush to the top of the front rail with biscuits and glue. It is approximately 1½ in. wider (¾ in. on each side) than the front rail and ¾ in. deeper than the inside of the case to fit into its dadoes (see "Top Panel").

2. Do the same with the bottom panel and bottom front rail. The bottom front rail is a different shape, but the measurements are the same.

3. For doorstops, cut two ⅜-in.-square strips the same length as the front rails.

4. Drill and countersink for some small decorative screws that will be used to attach these pieces after the piece is assembled.

Dry-fitting the carcase

1. Dry-fit all the frames you have made and make any adjustments necessary. It's quite a sight when all the pieces come together, and it should give you a sense of accomplishment.

2. While everything is clamped tightly together, measure for the ⅜-in.-thick side and back panels.

3. Trim the panels to size.

4. Mark where the dadoes in the side and back rails that will house the top and bottom meet the rear corner posts. Chop out this corner with a mallet and chisel when you take the piece apart.

5. Measure the space for the doors. It's important that the doors fit the opening well. The best way to be sure of this is to size them exactly from the actual opening.

6. Leave the case clamped up dry and go on to making the doors.

MAKING THE DOORS

Cutting the joints on the rails and stiles

Generally speaking, door joinery should be as strong as you can make it. Unlike the carcase joints, which have to be shallow so that two can fit in the post at right angles to each

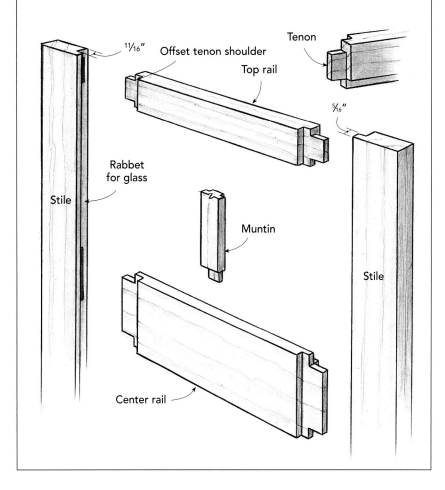

DOOR FRAME CONSTRUCTION

The door frames are simply mortised and tenoned together. The tenon shoulders are offset to compensate for the rabbet that houses the glass panes.

Stile
¹¹⁄₁₆"
Offset tenon shoulder
Top rail
Tenon
⁵⁄₁₆"
Rabbet for glass
Muntin
Stile
Center rail

other, the door joints can be much deeper. And they need to be because the doors have a lot more stress on them and glass panes are much heavier than wood panels (see "Door Frame Construction").

1. Cut ⁵⁄₁₆-in. by ¹¹⁄₁₆-in. rabbets for the glass panes on the inside back edges of the rails and stiles and the back of both long edges of the center rails. Use a dado cutter on your table saw.

2. Lay out and cut 1-in.-deep mortises for the rails.

Photo G: The sequence of table-saw cuts in the muntins begins (left to right) with two rips to create the rabbet, two more in a tenoning jig to form the faces of the tenon, two crosscuts to determine the shoulders of the tenon, and several more crosscuts to create the half-lap.

Photo H: The door parts in this exploded view show the relationship of the parts.

Tip: Dado cutters can catch and throw small parts, so use a rip blade and take many passes when the piece is small.

3. Cut the tenons using the same method as for the carcase joints, sizing them to their mortises. With the offset shoulder, they look different, but the techniques to make them are the same.

Making and joining the muntins

1. Check the fit of each door frame joint between rail and stile.

2. Dry-clamp the doors, and measure for the muntins, or center rails and stiles, which make up the top section of each door.

3. Make pieces out of 1-in.-square stock, half-lap them together in the center, and mortise them into the surrounding frame.

4. Cut two $\frac{5}{16}$-in. rabbets for the glass in these pieces in two rips on the table saw, with each rip defining a side of the rabbet. You'll end up with $\frac{3}{8}$ in. of stock in the middle, which defines one side of the $\frac{3}{8}$-in. by $\frac{3}{8}$-in. tenon (see **photo G**).

5. Cut the tenons using the same table-saw jig used in the "Simple Short Bookcase" (see p. 25). The jig holds the workpiece on end as you make two cuts, defining the remaining sides of the $\frac{3}{8}$-in.-square tenon. Cut these at two different heights for the different shoulders that accommodate the rabbet for the glass, just like the other door tenons.

6. Cut the cheeks of these tenons using the miter gauge to guide the workpieces.

7. To cut the half-lap joint that connects these pieces to form the cross, set your rip fence to half the length of the muntins.

8. Set the sawblade to the appropriate height (depending on which piece you're cutting).

9. Use your miter gauge to guide the muntin, registering one end of the workpiece against the fence.

10. Make two cuts for each fence setting and nibble away at the lap, moving the fence a bit at a time until the parts fit together. The joint has to be exactly in the center of the workpiece.

11. Lay out the mortise locations for the muntin cross. Ideally the mortises should be in the center of the top and center rails and centered in the sides between the top and center rails. Just in case they're not, use the completed cross to locate each mortise.

12. Take apart the door frames and cut the mortises. One plunge with a ⅜-in. bit in a hollow-chisel mortiser and you're set. Beware: the mortise for a tenon this small has to be located very precisely; if you have to trim to make it fit, it will throw the panes out of square.

13. Dry-fit the whole door assembly to make sure it all goes together (see **photo H**).

14. Glue and clamp up the doors and set them aside to dry.

Assembling and dry-installing the doors

For door hardware, use BC-275 bullet catches on the top and bottom and #ST-80, ½-in. straight knife hinges to hang the doors because they can't be seen when the doors are closed. Both are available from Larry & Faye Brusso Company (see Sources on pp. 182-183). If you use an offset knife hinge, the installation will be easier, but you'll have to patina the hinges to match the hardware with AS1 Antiquing Solution, available from Whitechapel Ltd. (see Sources).

1. Sand the doors smooth.

2. Fit the doors to the clamped-up case. Cut the doors so there's a gap of about ³⁄₃₂ in. around the edges and between the doors.

3. Lay out the hinge and catch locations on the doors.

4. Drill for the ball catches and mortise for the hinges. Do this now before the case is finally assembled because the hinges and the catches are extremely difficult to fit after the case is together.

5. Temporarily shim the doors evenly in their openings and mark the hinge and catch locations on the case.

6. Carefully mark the locations of the hinge side of the doors onto the inside of the front corner posts. This is important, because the use of knife hinges requires that the inside edges of these posts be relieved to allow the edge of the doors to clear the posts as they open (see "Clearance for Door Swing").

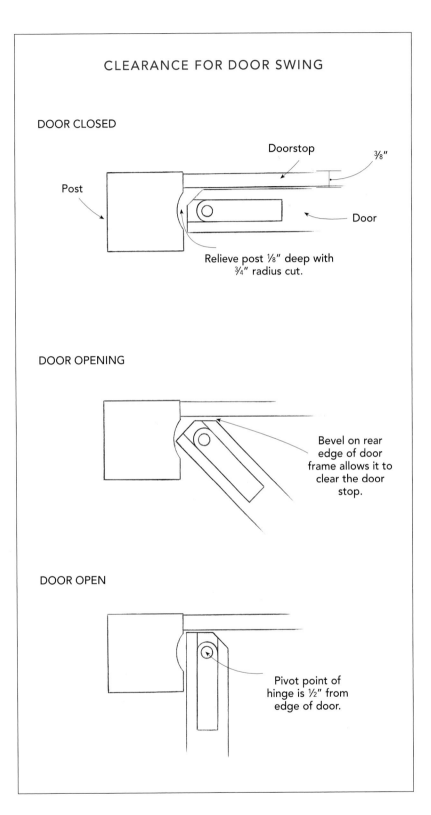

CLEARANCE FOR DOOR SWING

DOOR CLOSED

Post

Doorstop

⅜"

Door

Relieve post ⅛" deep with ¾" radius cut.

DOOR OPENING

Bevel on rear edge of door frame allows it to clear the door stop.

DOOR OPEN

Pivot point of hinge is ½" from edge of door.

Photo I: Rout the waste out of the knife-hinge mortise, and clean up the edges with a chisel.

Photo J: The bullet catches sit in two aligned holes in the door and case.

REAMY GLASS

Rodel recommends using hand-blown Reamy glass in the doors instead of hardware-store plate glass to give the entire piece a period look. Reamy glass is blown in a cylinder, then cut, opened flat, and allowed to cool. It is slightly wavy and uneven in its thickness with occasional bubbles.

Reamy glass is available from art-glass suppliers. There can be a lot of variation in the look, so it's best to pick it out in person.

7. Take apart the case, and using a ¾-in. core-box bit set to a depth of a little over ⅛ in. in a router table, rout a flute in the inside edges of the front corner posts. This is to allow the door to swing on the knife hinges. Be sure to stop this flute just beyond where the door ends or it will show.
8. Relieve the back edge of the hinge side of each door with a bevel so it will clear the doorstop.
9. Mortise for the hinges and drill for the catches (see **photos I** and **J**).

Making the glass stops
1. Size and buy glass panes for the doors (see "Reamy Glass").
2. Rip some stock for stops to keep the glass panes in place. The size of these stops depends on the thickness of the glass you use.

DETAIL WORK AND FINAL ASSEMBLY

Making and applying the inlay in the front posts
With the lion's share of the joinery completed, move on to the decorative work on the posts. This should be completed before assembly because it's easier to work with the posts on their own than it is with an assembled carcase. I do the inlay at this point because it's a lot of work. If I do it earlier, and then make a mistake (yes, I make mistakes) cutting the joinery and have to make a new post, I'd waste a lot of time. Of course, this strategy doesn't ensure against serious mistakes made while inlaying, but it's a smaller risk.

Half-Scale Layout of Inlay

Photocopy the drawing at 200 percent, for a set of full-size plans to lay out your template.

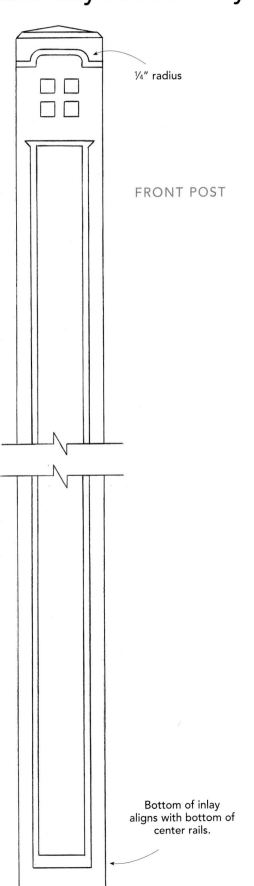

¼" radius

FRONT POST

Bottom of inlay aligns with bottom of center rails.

UPPER BACK RAIL

1" radius

ROUTER INLAY KIT

If you haven't done inlay before, use a router inlay kit available from Whiteside Machine & Repair Company (see Sources on pp. 182-183). It will help you enormously. Just follow the instructions and go slowly.

The kit is designed primarily for inlayed shapes such as the square ones in this project. It will produce both the negative shape (the hole to accept the inlay) and the positive shape (the inlay itself).

I also like the kit for line work, though you can't use it the same way because the positive for thin-line inlay is too delicate to cut with this system. The kit comes with the smallest guide bushing I have been able to find. It also comes with one of the nicest router bits of its kind on the market and decent instructions.

Everything you need to inlay, from top to bottom: templates for several shapes, clamps, and a router with a ⅛-in. up-cut spiral bit and guide bushing; chisel and knife for cutting corner details; corner post, full-size plans, and strips of ⅛-in. inlay. Glue is not included.

Tip: Don't get too carried away sanding the outside of the piece at this point because it will surely get a few dings and scratches during glue-up.

Photo K: Ebony wedges should be hammered into their kerfs evenly and at the same time.

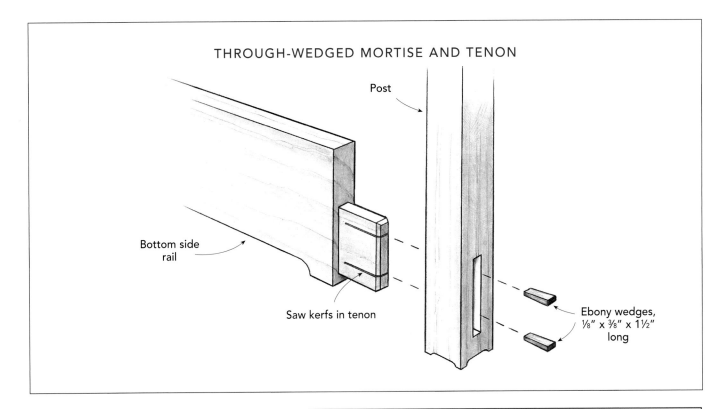

THROUGH-WEDGED MORTISE AND TENON

Post

Bottom side
rail

Saw kerfs in tenon

Ebony wedges,
⅛" x ⅜" x 1½"
long

1. Make a template for the inlay shapes from the half-scale patterns shown in "Half-Scale Layout of Inlay" on p. 127.
2. Rout the grooves with a ⅛-in. straight down-cut spiral bit and a small bushing (see "Router Inlay Kit").
3. Square up the corners with a chisel.
4. Cut and glue the ebony inlay in place.

Carcase assembly and glue-up

Though the bookcase still looks like a pile of parts, you are really close to being finished at this point. Preassemble some of the sections before the overall glue-up to cut down on the confusion. Still, it will be helpful to have another person available during final glue-up because it's a little tricky and you need to move fairly fast.

1. Finish-sand to 180 grit all the parts difficult to access after assembly.
2. Glue up the sides, connecting the corner posts with the rails and capturing the panels. Spread a little glue on the through tenon wedges and tap them home (see **photo K** and "Through-Wedged Mortise and Tenon").

USING GLUE

It's a good idea not to apply too much glue to the mortises and tenons. Excess glue that squeezes out is really difficult to clean from all the nooks and crannies in this piece, and you run the risk of glue invading the grooves that hold the panels. The panels have to float in their grooves. If they are accidentally glued in place, you risk panels splitting or joints being compromised.

3. Assemble the back, except for the posts.
4. Glue up the top, bottom, and center rails to their connecting stiles, including the center panels, and set all these parts aside to dry (see "Using Glue").
5. Glue the dry subassemblies together into a full carcase, starting by laying one side face down on an assembly bench.
6. Spread glue into the mortises for the top and bottom front rails, and insert the tenons. Leave the dadoes that hold the top and bottom dry so the top and bottom can move freely.

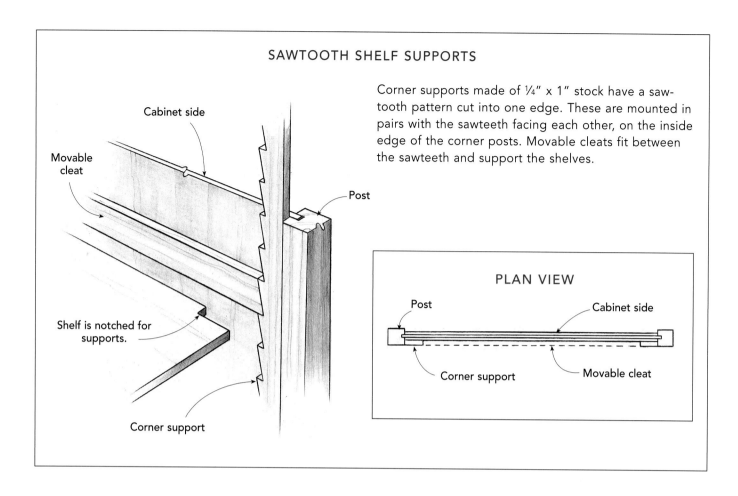

SAWTOOTH SHELF SUPPORTS

Corner supports made of ¼" x 1" stock have a saw-tooth pattern cut into one edge. These are mounted in pairs with the sawteeth facing each other, on the inside edge of the corner posts. Movable cleats fit between the sawteeth and support the shelves.

Cabinet side

Movable cleat

Post

Shelf is notched for supports.

Corner support

PLAN VIEW

Post

Cabinet side

Corner support

Movable cleat

Tip: This bookcase is pretty much self-squaring because there are so many joints holding it that way. But it's always prudent to check as you go and clamp across diagonals to correct the angles if possible.

7. Move quickly to the back, slide in the remaining panels, spread glue into the mortises for the back rails, and insert these tenons. Again, leave the dadoes in the back for the top and bottom dry.

8. Spread glue into all the mortises in the other side, place it on its mating tenons and start clamping the case together. You can see why some extra hands are welcome.

9. Drill and countersink holes through to the bottom, front, and back rail tenons, insert some screws, put a little glue in the screw holes, and fill the holes with small square ebony plugs.

10. Finish-sand the outside of the piece when the glue has dried, and lightly break all the corners.

11. Cut the tenon wedges flush with the tenon and bevel it slightly.

12. Bevel the screw plugs just above the surface.

13. Gently round and soften the through-wedged tenons and the plugs by hand-sanding.

Fitting the shelves

There are three adjustable shelves in this bookcase, but because of their locations, they are two different widths.

1. Measure for the top shelf. It stays hidden behind the center rails of the doors, putting it between the center rails of the sides. Measure between these locations, subtract about ³⁄₃₂ in., and cut it to length.

2. Measure for the bottom two shelves. They rest between the lower side panels and are consequently a little longer. Subtract ³⁄₃₂ in., then cut the shelves to length.

3. Measure the shelf depths and rip them down to size. The shelves should fit just behind the front corner posts. They should also be a hair smaller than the interior spaces

so they'll fit without being forced and have room to move seasonally.

4. Rout a ¼-in. cove in the bottom front edge of each shelf. This looks like and is done just like the cove in the upper front rail.

5. Notch the ends of the shelves around the support-system rails, leaving enough room for them to move seasonally (but do this after the rails are made and installed).

Adjustable shelf-support system

The last thing to make is the adjustable shelf-support system. I use an old system of corner supports and movable cleats (see **photo L** and "Sawtooth Shelf Supports"). The short strip that supports the top shelf is positioned to allow the shelf about 3 in. of adjustment and still keep it behind the center rails of the doors. Glue the corner supports to the posts so they don't interfere with any movement of the panels.

FINISHING UP

Rodel recommends a pure linseed oil product called Tried and True Varnish Oil (see Sources on pp. 182-183) manufactured by the Robson Family in Trumansburg, New York. It produces a fine finish and imparts a wonderful color and glow to the cherry. It is also non-toxic and contains no petroleum distillates, derivatives, or metal dryers, which is something that can't be said about many finishes on the market today.

1. Finish the bookcase with whatever finish you prefer.

2. Install the glass and hang the doors.

3. Install the doorstops. In case there are any minor issues with the way the doors hang, you can reposition the stops slightly to accommodate any needed changes.

4. Install the door pulls. I used an Arts and Crafts style pull called Pacific Style #C3451 (also recommended by Kevin Rodel), available from Craftsman Hardware (see Sources).

BARRISTER BOOKCASE

I have always liked the idea of the barrister, or lawyer's, bookcase. The stacking modules have a versatile appeal and seem really practical. The glass doors protect and display books or other cherished items and tuck out of the way when open. On the other hand, the first ones I saw years ago at auctions and tag sales had an array of complicated mechanisms designed for the simple process of sliding the doors out of the way, and they never seemed to function very well. And most fit together poorly and always appeared in danger of toppling.

Curtis Erpelding, a professional woodworker and designer in Port Orchard, Wash., who built the original of this bookcase, apparently felt the same way. Unlike me, he did something about it. The result is an elegant, updated bookcase that's a vast improvement on the auction variety. The door mechanism and the method for stacking the boxes together work really well and are marvelously simple.

This piece was conceived as a possible production item, so a lot of parts and procedures are standardized. The doors and frames are joined with bridle joints, and the case is biscuited together. The parts are also dimensioned so that one sheet of plywood and 25 bd. ft. of 8/4 lumber will produce one complete three-stage unit.

This barrister bookcase knocks down into case sections, a top, and a base.

Barrister Bookcase

THIS STACKING BOOKCASE consists of three basic elements: three cases with glass doors that pivot up and slide into the case when open, a top, and a base. The base is a mitered and biscuited frame. The top is a simple plywood panel with solid-wood edging. The cases consist of a top and bottom frame built with bridle joints biscuited into plywood sides and a back. The cases stack neatly on top of each other by means of registration splines. The doors are built with bridle joints and hold glass panes.

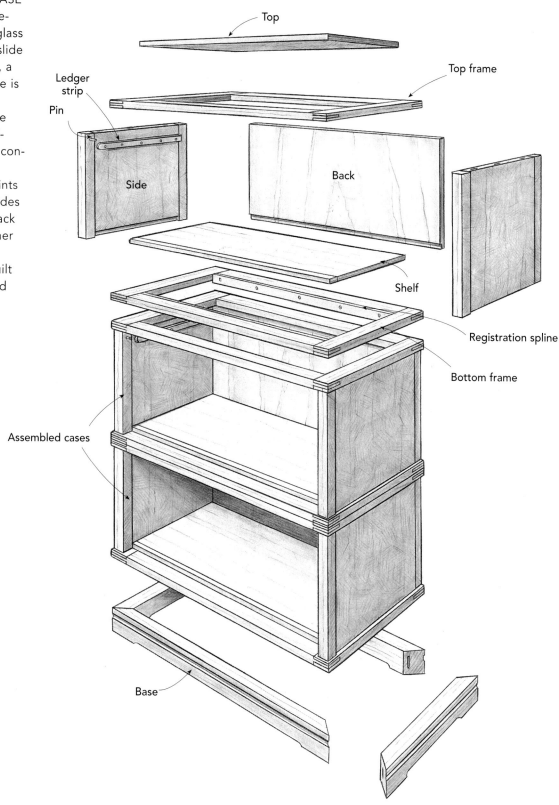

Top

Top frame

Ledger strip

Pin

Side

Back

Shelf

Registration spline

Bottom frame

Assembled cases

Base

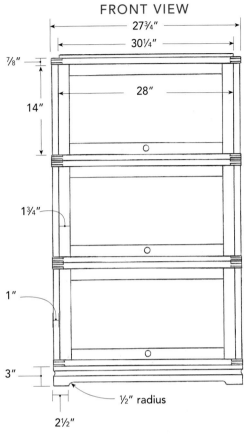

FRONT VIEW

27¾"
30¼"

⅞"
14"
28"
1¾"
1"
3"
½" radius
2½"

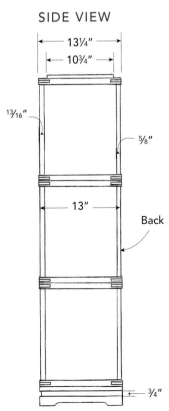

SIDE VIEW

13¼"
10¾"
13/16"
⅝"
13"
Back
¾"

CUT LIST FOR BARRISTER BOOKCASE

Cases

12	Frame members	30⅜ in. x 1¾ in. x ⅞ in.
12	Frame members	13⅜ in. x 1¾ in. x ⅞ in.
6	Sides	14 in. x 11⁹⁄₁₆ in. x ¾ in., vertical-grain Douglas fir plywood
3	Backs	14 in. x 28 in. x ¾ in., vertical-grain Douglas fir plywood
6	Edging for front of sides	14 in. x 1 in. x ¹³⁄₁₆ in.
6	Edging for back of sides	14 in. x ¾ in. x ⅝ in.
3	Bottoms (shelves)	28¼ in. x 11⁹⁄₁₆ in. x ¾ in., vertical-grain Douglas fir plywood
3	Edging for shelf fronts	28¼ in. x ¾ in. x ¼ in.
6	Registration strips	26¾ in. x 1¼ in. x ¼ in.

Doors

6	Door rails	28⅛ in. x 1¾ in. x ¾ in.
6	Door stiles	14⅛ in. x 1¾ in. x ¾ in.
6	Ledger strips	11¼ in. x 1 in. x ¼ in.

Door Hardware

6	Brass shelf pins	¼ in.
3	Small brass knobs	

Base

2	Base members	30¼ in. x 1¾ in. x 3 in.
2	Base members	13¼ in. x 1¾ in. x 3 in.

Top

1	Top	26¼ in. x 9¼ in. x ¾ in., vertical-grain Douglas fir plywood
2	Edging for top	27¾ in. x ¾ in. x ¾ in.
2	Edging for top	10¾ in. x ¾ in. x ¾ in.

All parts are solid Douglas fir except where otherwise indicated.

BUILDING THE BOOKCASE STEP-BY-STEP

BECAUSE THIS PIECE was designed for production, the parts are as simple as possible. Many parts share common joinery, and the details are very simple. Everything is joined with biscuits or bridle joints. The cases take the most work, so it makes sense to build them first.

MAKING THE CASES

Making the case frames

The frames that become the top and bottom of each section of this bookcase are joined with bridle joints, sometimes called slot or open mortise-and-tenon joints.

1. Mill the stock for the six case frames to the dimensions on the cut list.

2. Crosscut the parts ⅛ in. longer than finished length so you can trim the joints flush after they're assembled.

3. To cut the half-laps, use a handsaw or a table-saw tenoning jig. I use an Inca tenoning jig on my table saw to cut these joints, but the shopmade jig on p. 25 works as well.

4. Set your table-saw blade height to the width of the frame members plus ¹⁄₁₆ in.

5. Make two cuts to form the faces of the mortise in the side pieces. Then nibble away the waste in between by making multiple passes across the sawblade (see **photo A**).

6. With the blade set to the same height as the mortise cuts, make the tenon cheek cuts in the other frame members (see **photo B**).

7. Cut the shoulder of the tenons with the workpiece lying flat on the table saw and guided through the cut by a miter gauge. Lower the blade so it just enters the kerf produced by the cheek cuts (see **photo C**).

8. Test-fit the joints and fine-tune them until they're just right (see "Bridle Joint Fit").

9. Glue and place clamps across the frame in both directions and as close to the joints as possible—but not directly over them—and pull the joints together tightly.

10. With these clamps still in place, position a clamp at each corner to hold the joints together. Check for square and adjust accordingly.

11. Remove the first clamps. The ends of the joints sit a little proud at this point, a result of overcutting the joint slightly.

12. When the joints are dry, plane the ends flush with the sides of the frames using a sharp block plane. Make sure you cut toward the center of the frame, not toward the edge, to avoid tearout at the corners (see **photo D**).

Photo A: To mortise, first cut kerfs that form the outside faces of the mortise, then make multiple passes in between them to cut away the waste.

Photo B: To cut the tenons, use the same technique you did for the mortises, but don't take multiple passes to cut away the waste.

Photo C: The blade should be just high enough to remove the tenon waste when you cut the shoulders.

BRIDLE JOINT FIT

Though bridle joints are easy to make, I can't stress enough the importance of a good fit between mortise and tenon. All of us know that we can't get away with a loose joint, so we force ourselves to fix it or remake the parts. But a too-tight bridle joint is tempting to let slide because you can force it together without too much trouble. Take the time to get the right fit.

I could wax philosophical about the virtues of the perfect fit, but the simple fact is that taking a shortcut here will haunt you for the rest of the job with problems such as splitting or twisting of the frames. Trust me on this!

Photo D: A sharp, low-angle block plane will smooth the ends of the bridle joints flush with the sides.

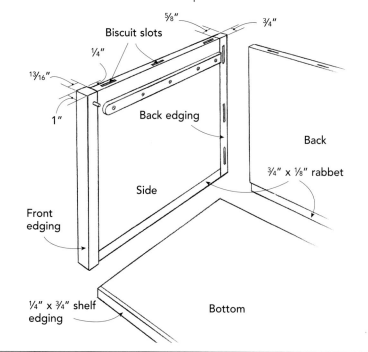

RELATIONSHIP OF EDGING TO SIDES AND RABBETS

The edging sizes are all calculated to make the box edges and rabbets line up when assembled.

⅝"

¾"

Biscuit slots

¼"

¹³/₁₆"

1"

Back edging

Back

Side

¾" x ⅛" rabbet

Front edging

¼" x ¾" shelf edging

Bottom

Photo E: Clamp a fence along the line where the side intersects the frame to guide the biscuit joiner.

Making the case sides, backs, and bottoms

1. Size all the plywood parts at one time, including the shelves (which serve as bottoms of the cases) and the top panel.

2. Cut ⅛-in.-deep by ¾-in.-wide rabbets on the bottom inside edge of the sides and back. These rabbets will later house the shelves. Cut these rabbets on the table saw by making a single pass over a ⅛-in.-wide sawblade set to a height of ¾ in., with the plywood parts standing on edge.

3. Mill four strips of solid-wood edging about 4 ft. long. Two are ¹³/₁₆ in. by 1 in. for the front edges of the sides and two are ⅝ in. by ¾ in. for the back edges.

4. Cut these strips into three pieces each and attach them to their respective edges with biscuits and glue.

5. Attach the front edges so they are flush with the inside faces and overhang the outside faces of the sides by ¼ in. The ¹³/₁₆-in. face will allow the doors, once installed, to be recessed ¹/₁₆ in. from the front edge of the sides.

6. Attach the ¾-in. face of the thinner strips to the back of the sides. This will become the back corner of the case, and it will also be attached by biscuits to the back (see "Relationship of Edging to Sides and Rabbets").

7. Glue and clamp these parts and set them aside to dry.

8. Rip and plane the ¼-in. by ¾-in. shelf edging, and glue and clamp it to the front edge of the shelves, or bottoms, of the cases.

9. Clean off any excess glue when dry and sand the assembled parts flush.

10. Lay out and cut the slots for the biscuits that will join the backs to the sides.

11. Lay out and cut biscuit slots in the top and bottom edges of the backs and sides that will join the top and bottom frames to these parts.

Tip: Register your biscuit joiner on the inside faces of the backs and sides in step 11 so when you do step 13, you'll have more surface area to rest your biscuit joiner.

Pivoting Door Mechanism

The entire mechanism relies on a pair of metal pins attached to the upper front corners of the sides. The pins ride in stopped grooves in the sides of the doors. A plain ledger strip supports each door in the open position.

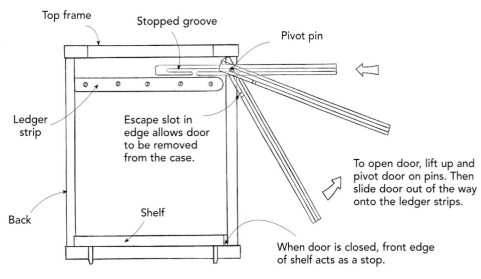

Top frame

Stopped groove

Pivot pin

Ledger strip

Escape slot in edge allows door to be removed from the case.

Back

Shelf

To open door, lift up and pivot door on pins. Then slide door out of the way onto the ledger strips.

When door is closed, front edge of shelf acts as a stop.

A simple pin and ledger strip are enough to guide and support the door in the open position.

When open, the door reveals the groove in the edge that rides on the pin in the case.

12. Dry-assemble the backs and sides, carefully positioning them on the frames, and mark a line along the inside edges on the frames for the location of the biscuit slots.

13. Clamp a piece of wood along this line and cut the mating slots in the frames, using the wood as a fence for the biscuit joiner (see **photo E**).

14. Dry-fit all these parts to make sure everything fits well. Then disassemble everything.

Making the door mechanism

The door mechanism that Erpelding devised for this bookcase couldn't be simpler. When he first described it to me I reacted the same way I do when I find a parking spot in New York City: It seems too good to be true, therefore something must be wrong with it. I found, however, that it's the genuine article. There are no complex hidden springs, counterweights, or wire to entangle or befuddle you (see "Pivoting Door Mechanism").

1. Locate the center for the pivot-pin hole 1 in. down from the top and ⁷⁄₁₆ in. in from the front edge. The distance down from the top allows room for you to get the doors on and off the pins. The pin's distance in from the front edge is ¹⁄₁₆ in. greater than half the thickness of the door. When the doors are shut, they are recessed the same ¹⁄₁₆ in.

Photo F: Assemble the sides and back of the case before you set them into the frames because it's not possible to do it any other way.

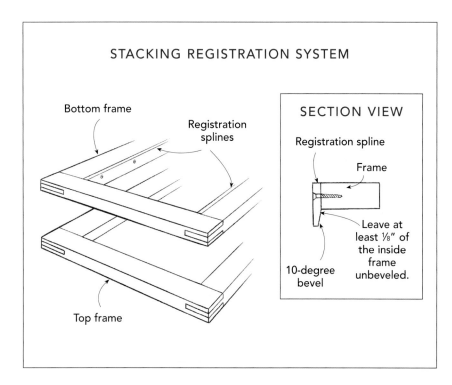

STACKING REGISTRATION SYSTEM

Bottom frame

Registration splines

Top frame

SECTION VIEW

Registration spline

Frame

Leave at least ⅛" of the inside frame unbeveled.

10-degree bevel

2. Drill a ¼-in. hole ¾ in. deep, and tap in a ¼-in. shelf pin such as you would use for an adjustable shelf on another bookcase.

3. Make two ledger strips for each case 1 in. by ¼ in. by 11¼ in. Round the front edge of each so they won't mar the doors or interfere with their closing.

4. Position each ledger strip flush with the back and 1½ in. down from the top of the side. The distance down from the top puts it ⅛ in. below the horizontal position of the door when open. If it were higher, the door might tend to slide forward and close by itself.

5. Use some decorative brass screws to install the strips.

Assembling the cases and attaching the registration strips

1. Finish-sand all the parts to 180 grit.

2. Glue and clamp the backs to the sides (see **photo F**).

3. One at a time, lay a top frame on the bench and glue the back and sides to the frame.

4. Install the shelf into the rabbets in the back and sides. Don't use any glue here because once the case is fully assembled, the bottom can't go anywhere. It's sandwiched between the bottom frame and the rabbets in the sides and back.

5. Glue on the bottom frame and clamp the assembly top to bottom at each biscuit location. Do this for each of the three cases, one at a time.

6. Mill up 1¼-in. by ¼-in. registration strips and bevel one face 10 degrees.

7. When the glue on the cases has dried, screw or glue and clamp the registration strips to the inside edges of the bottom frame of each case, both in the front and the back (see "Stacking Registration System").

Making the doors

The basic construction of the door is the same as the frames. However, since the doors have to hold a pane of glass, the inside edges are rabbeted (see **photo G**). The only other difference is that the doors are ¾ in. thick, while the frames are ⅞ in. thick. I also wait until the cases are complete to fit them (see "Fitting Doors to the Case").

FITTING DOORS TO THE CASE

When building a piece of furniture that includes doors, I feel it's prudent to wait until the case is fully assembled before I mill the parts to size. This way, I can size the parts to the actual, rather than the theoretical, opening. This is particularly important when the tolerances between the door and case are critical to the proper operation of the door, as is the case here.

Photo G: The door frames have a rabbet along the inside edge to house the glass. Otherwise, their construction is identical to the case frames.

1. Cut a ½-in. by ½-in. rabbet in one long edge of each of the door members on the table saw using a dado cutter. The size of this rabbet places the weight of the glass slightly forward of the pivot point of the door, which is enough to keep the door closed without the use of a catch. If the weight of the glass were behind the pivot point, the doors would hang slightly open and a catch would be necessary.
2. Machine the joints for the doors using the same jig you used earlier on the table saw.
3. Glue and clamp the door frames together, making sure they're square and not twisted.
4. While the glue is drying, rip and plane some ⅜-in.-square stock for later use as glass stops.

Grooving the door sides for the door mechanism

Cut the stopped grooves in the sides of the doors on a router table to complete the door mechanism.

1. Plane the dry door joints flush and sand all the joints flat.
2. Using a ¼-in. straight bit, rout a groove ⅜ in. deep exactly in the center of the edge of both sides of all the doors.
3. Stop the groove ⅞ in. from the top of each door.
4. Clamp a stop block to the router table fence, using a piece of scrap the same size as

USING DOUGLAS FIR

This piece is built of Douglas fir, both solid wood and plywood. Erpelding has a soft spot for the wood. Some of his first attempts at furniture, he says, were made from construction-grade Douglas fir, and over the years he has come to appreciate it more and more. It's lightness and contemporary look made it the perfect choice for this bookcase.

The sides and backs are made of vertical-grain Douglas fir plywood. This plywood simply has a veneer that is sliced in such a way as to produce very straight, parallel grain. It is not the most common face veneer for plywood. It may be hard for you to obtain, and it's somewhat expensive.

Veneering a sheet of plywood is an option, if the idea doesn't intimidate you. I found that vertical-grain Douglas fir veneer was available from all the veneer suppliers I called. Failing all this, you could certainly build this piece in some other more easily available species such as cherry, maple, or oak.

a door edge as a test piece to position this stop exactly.
5. Starting at what will be the bottom edge of the door, pass the door edge across the router bit to the stop block, then lift it carefully off the router bit (see "Routing the Door Grooves" on p. 142).

Routing the Door Grooves

1. Rout groove in edge of door.

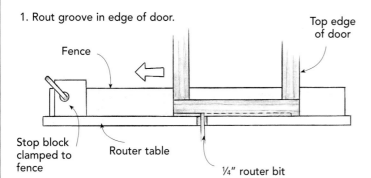

Fence

Top edge of door

Stop block clamped to fence

Router table

¼" router bit

2. Lift door up at end of cut to leave last ⅞" uncut.

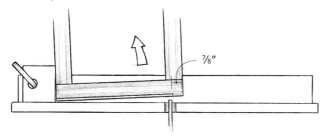

⅞"

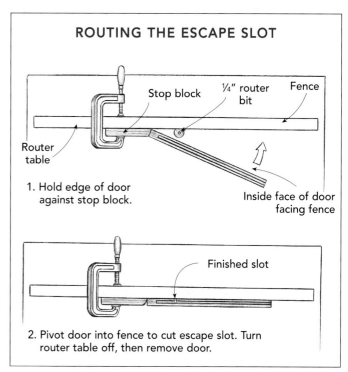

ROUTING THE ESCAPE SLOT

Stop block

¼" router bit

Fence

Router table

1. Hold edge of door against stop block.

Inside face of door facing fence

Finished slot

2. Pivot door into fence to cut escape slot. Turn router table off, then remove door.

MITER ZEN

If you've ever tried getting frame miters just right—and I mean just right—you know how frustrating it can be. Tools that are out of alignment by a hair can still leave a noticeable gap in the joint. Fussing with them often seems to make the joint even worse.

Cutting miters accurately requires what I call "miter zen." This is the art of feeling your way through a fit, knowing the ways in which you or your tools cut slightly off the mark or break out, and compensating for these errors in such ways that the joint comes out right, and without fuss. Rather than fight the accumulated errors of each tool you use, you try to foresee their inaccuracies and work with them to end up with a perfect joint. After all, 44½ degrees is just as precise and difficult an angle to cut as 45 degrees.

6. To form the escape slot, reposition the stop block 3 in. from the router bit. Using it as a pivot point, place the top of the door against it (with the inside face of the door toward the fence) and swing the door into the fence and across the bit. This method will cut the slot in a controlled manner (see "Routing the Escape Slot").

7. Put a slight radius, or rounded bevel, on the top front edge of the doors so they clear the bottom of the top frames when pivoting.

8. Finish-sand the doors and install them in their cases.

TOP AND BASE

Milling and assembling the top and base

The top is simply a plywood panel with a mitered solid-wood frame to hide the edges. Cutting the miters can be tricky to get right: Test-fit everything before you glue it together (see "Miter Zen").

Photo H: Clamp the bottom edges of two base sections and drill a 1-in. hole between them to form the half-round corners at the ends of the cutout.

Photo I: Bandsaw the waste between the half-rounds to create the base detail.

1. Using a ½-in. piloted rabbeting bit set to a depth of ¼ in., rout a rabbet around all four sides of the top panel so it will sit into the top frame, projecting up ½ in.

2. Mill some 1¾-in. by 3-in. stock for the base.

3. Using a ¾-in.-diameter corebox bit in a router table, rout a ¾-in. flute 1⅞ in. up from the bottom edge to the centerline (see "Base Construction").

4. Cut the base front, back, and side pieces to length.

5. Clamp the base pieces together in pairs, making sure they are flush on top and bottom.

6. Draw a line across each pair 3 in. from each end. At the point this line intersects the line where these pieces join is the center for a 1-in.-diameter hole (see **photo H**).

7. Drill the holes with a Forstner bit. When the pairs are separated again, these holes form the curve at each end of the base cutout.

8. Finish the cutout on a bandsaw, connecting the two half holes (see **photo I**). Sand off the bandsaw marks.

9. Miter the ends of each base piece and cut a biscuit slot for each corner.

10. Glue and clamp the base together.

Finishing Douglas fir

In my opinion, the only way to bring out the depth of color inherent in Douglas fir is

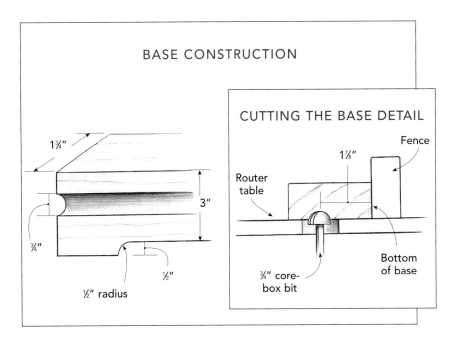

BASE CONSTRUCTION

1¾"

3"

¾"

½"

½" radius

CUTTING THE BASE DETAIL

Fence

1⅞"

Router table

Bottom of base

¾" corebox bit

with oil. I used my old standby, Watco Danish Oil finish. The downside to most oil finishes is that they are not permanent. They dry out, wear, and have to be periodically reapplied. If this is to happen, they have to be easy to apply, and Watco fits the bill. Initial finishing takes a few coats, but reapplication is just a matter of wiping on a coat, wiping off the excess, and then letting it dry.

After finishing I install the glass in the doors. Using the glass stops I cut earlier, I carefully cut and fit them into the rabbets and attach them with small brads.

Formal Sideboard Bookcase

This bookcase was part of a series of furniture I built for a client in an apartment. Like a lot of apartment furniture, functionally the bookcase had to do double duty.

First, it had to store large-format art books and photo albums. Second, it was to be placed against a wall just outside the dining alcove, and would also serve as a sideboard. This is why it has a low profile and a large granite top. Because it had to hold silverware, place mats, and napkins, drawers were a necessity. Finally, when not used as a sideboard during meals, the clients wanted to display family photographs on the top.

Integrating all these uses into a single piece of furniture so it looked right for each purpose was a challenge. I worked with interior designer David Hecht on the design of the piece. We decided on quite a mix of materials, including mahogany, ash, cherry plywood, birch plywood, walnut burl veneer, black granite, and gold leaf.

The result is a relatively formal piece with a modern design edge. I wouldn't exactly call it low-key, but it doesn't scream at you either. In any case, what's really important is that, even with all that's going on, it fulfills its role as everyday furniture.

Formal Sideboard Bookcase

THOUGH LOADED WITH DETAILS, this bookcase is simple in construction. At heart, it's a biscuit-joined plywood carcase. Added onto this are a granite top, drawers with veneered fronts, mahogany face and side frames, and winged feet.

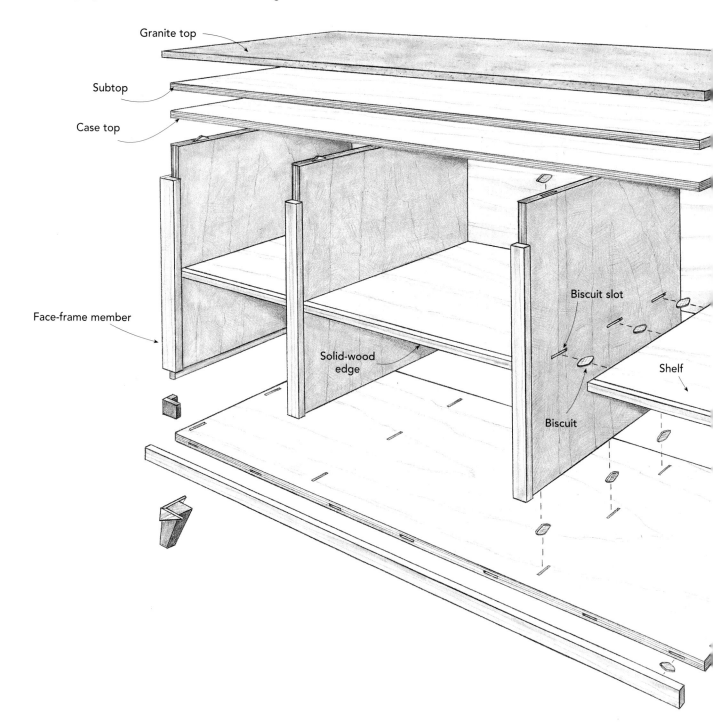

Granite top

Subtop

Case top

Face-frame member

Solid-wood edge

Biscuit slot

Biscuit

Shelf

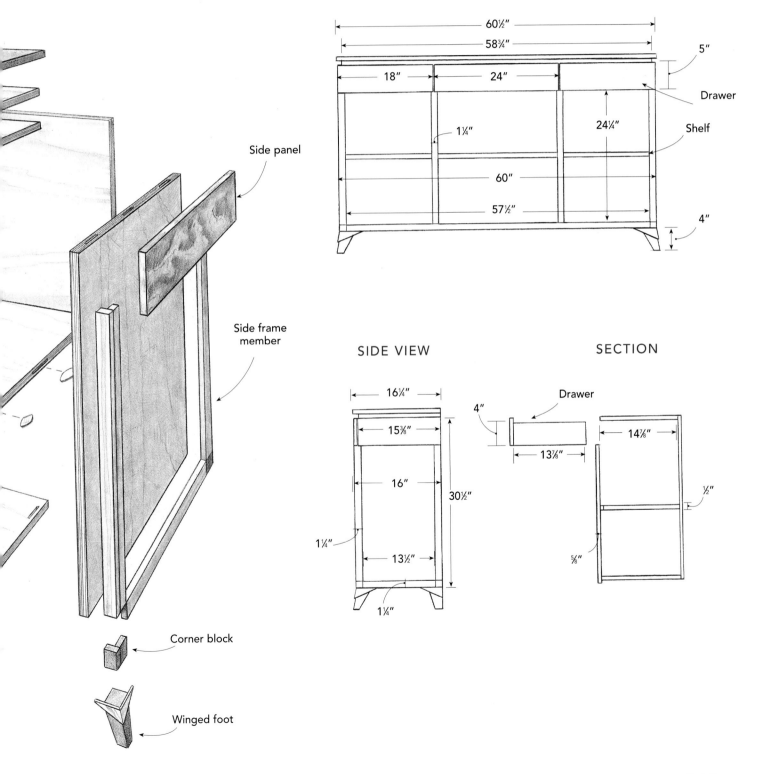

MEASURED DRAWING

60½"

58¾"

5"

18"   24"   Drawer

1¼"   24¼"   Shelf

60"

57½"

4"

SIDE VIEW

16¼"

15⅜"

16"   30½"

1¼"

13½"

1¼"

Side panel

Side frame
member

Corner block

Winged foot

SECTION

Drawer

4"

13⅞"   14⅞"

½"

⅝"

BUILDING THE BOOKCASE STEP-BY-STEP

CHERRY, MAHOGANY, walnut burl veneer, black granite, and gold leaf: That's quite a list of materials. Add a face frame that connects with a faux frame and panel on the side, drawers with veneered fronts that appear to wrap around the sides, corner blocks, and odd splayed feet, and you might begin to wonder if there isn't too much going on in this bookcase. Looking back at the job, I've had my doubts. But the construction is extremely simple. This project is fundamentally a large, biscuit-joined, plywood box, onto which a variety of details are attached (see "Carcase Construction" on p. 150).

CUT LIST FOR FORMAL SIDEBOARD BOOKCASE

Carcase and Shelves

2	Sides	28½ in. x 14⅞ in. x ¾ in., cherry veneered plywood
2	Dividers	28½ in. x 14⅞ in. x ¾ in., cherry veneered plywood
1	Top	59 in. x 14⅞ in. x ¾ in., cherry veneered plywood
1	Bottom	59 in. x 14⅞ in. x ¾ in., cherry veneered plywood
1	Back	59 in. x 30 in. x ½ in., cherry veneered plywood
2	Shelves	16⅜ in. x 14⅜ in. x ¾ in., cherry veneered plywood
1	Shelf	23¼ in. x 14⅜ in. x ¾ in., cherry veneered plywood
1	Shelf edging	23¼ in. x ¾ in. x ½ in., solid mahogany
2	Shelf edging	16⅜ in. x ¾ in. x ½ in., solid mahogany

Face and Side Frames

4	Face frame stiles	24¼ in. x 1¼ in. x ⅝ in., solid mahogany
1	Face frame bottom rail	57½ in. x 1¼ in. x ⅝ in., solid mahogany
2	Corner frame stile pieces	24¼ in. x 1¼ in. x ⅝ in., solid mahogany
2	Corner frame stile pieces	24¼ in. x ⅝ in. x ½ in., solid mahogany
2	Side frame bottom rails	13½ in. x 1¼ in. x ½ in., solid mahogany
2	Side panels	15⅜ in. x 5 in. x 12mm, Baltic birch plywood

Feet

4	Feet	5 in. x 3 in. x 3 in., solid ash (oversize)
6	Wings for feet	5 in. x 2½ in. x 6mm, Baltic birch plywood (oversize)

CUT LIST FOR FORMAL SIDEBOARD BOOKCASE

Drawers

2	Drawer box fronts	14⅜ in. x 4 in. x 12mm, Baltic birch plywood
2	Drawer box backs	14⅜ in. x 3⅜ in. x 12mm, Baltic birch plywood
1	Drawer box front	21¼ in. x 4 in. x 12mm, Baltic birch plywood
1	Drawer box back	21¼ in. x 3⅜ in. x 12mm, Baltic birch plywood
6	Drawer sides	14 in. x 4 in. x 12mm, Baltic birch plywood
2	Drawer fronts	18 in. x 5 in. x 12mm, Baltic birch plywood
1	Drawer front	24 in. x 5 in. x 12mm, Baltic birch plywood
2	Drawer bottoms	14⅞ in. x 13¾ in. x 6mm, 5-ply Baltic birch plywood
1	Drawer bottom	21¾ in. x 13¾ in. x 6mm, 5-ply Baltic birch plywood

Top

1	Subtop	58¾ in. x 15¼ in. x ¾ in., maple or birch plywood
1	Top	60½ in. x 16¼ in. x ¾ in., black granite

Veneer

20 sq. ft.	walnut burl veneer for drawer fronts, corner blocks, and side return panels

Hardware

6	Drawer glides	14 in., full-extension Accuride 3832 series, black

I will describe some relatively uncommon techniques in this chapter, namely veneering and gilding. If you haven't tried either of these, you're missing out. Surface treatments such as these are like fabric to an upholsterer, and they open up a whole range of design possibilities. If not for this bookcase, learn them for their own sakes.

BUILDING THE CARCASE

Milling the parts and placing biscuit slots on the box

1. Rip the cherry plywood for the top, bottom, sides, dividers, and shelves to the same 14⅞-in. width, then crosscut the parts to their respective lengths.

2. Glue ½-in. by ¾-in. strips of mahogany to the front edges of the shelves.

3. After the glue is dry, sand the shelf edges flush.

4. Re-rip the shelves to the same 14⅞ in.

5. Lay out and cut all the biscuit slots (see pp. 38-41 for details on locating biscuit slots).

6. Finish-sand all the inside surfaces and glue, assemble, and clamp the case. Remember to check the diagonals after clamping.

7. When the glue dries, screw the ½-in. cherry plywood back flush with the top, bottom, and sides of the case. This will keep the case square as you work on it and provide a reference later for the parts that overhang the sides and top.

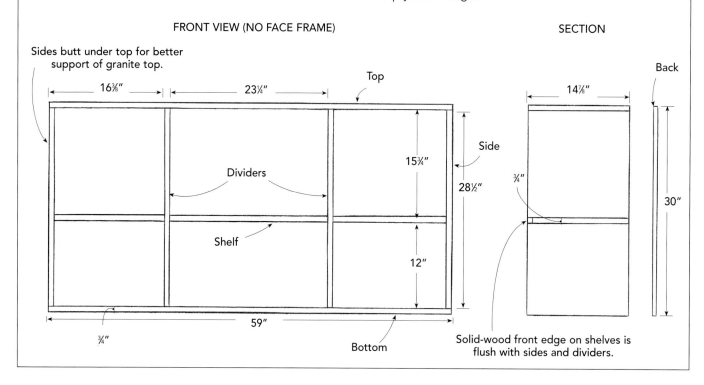

CARCASE CONSTRUCTION

The plywood case is nontraditional in two respects. The case is assembled with both the sides and dividers between the top and bottom to give better support for the downward weight of the granite top. The back is applied directly to the rear edges of the case, not into a rabbet. The side frame members, added later, cover the back's plywood edges.

FRONT VIEW (NO FACE FRAME)

SECTION

Sides butt under top for better support of granite top.

Back

16⅜"   23¼"

Top

14⅞"

¾"

Side

15¾"

Dividers

28½"

30"

Shelf

12"

59"

¾"

Bottom

Solid-wood front edge on shelves is flush with sides and dividers.

Attaching the face frame members

The face frame and side frames give the case a frame-and-panel look.

1. Mill all the mahogany parts for the face and side frames. These parts are all the same 1¼-in. width. The face frame parts are ⅝ in. thick, while the side frame pieces are ½ in. thick.

2. Cut them to length, and sand smooth any surfaces difficult to get to after assembly.

3. Finish-sand the sides of the case. It will be difficult to get to most of these areas after the frames are glued on.

4. Attach the bottom piece of face frame with biscuits, flush with the bottom of the case, extending below the carcase by ½ in. It should also be centered on the edge, ¾ in. shy of each end, to leave room for the corner blocks.

5. Mount the face frame members that cover the dividers on the center of each, overhanging them ¼ in. on each side and butted up against the bottom piece.

6. Glue and clamp on all the vertical members. Position them 5 in. short of the top of the case, leaving room for the veneered drawer fronts and side return panels. There's no need to biscuit these.

7. Position the top edge of the bottom side frame member ¾ in. up from the bottom edge, covering the exposed plywood, and ¾ in. shy of the front and back. Again, just glue and clamp it in place.

8. Glue and clamp the rear piece, overhanging the back of the case by ½ in. and ¾ in. up from the bottom, corner to corner with the bottom piece.

9. Glue and biscuit the corner members together, one piece ⅝ in. by 1¼ in. and one piece ⅝ in. by ½ in. These dimensions will make a corner that is equally wide on both sides (⅝ in. added to ⅝ in. equals 1¼ in.).
10. Position the corner members flush with the inside of the case, ¾ in. shy of the bottom edge of the carcase, and corner to corner with the bottom members on the side and front. Glue and clamp in place (see **photo A**).
11. Apply mahogany edge tape to the exposed plywood edges above the face frame. If you don't, the plywood edges will show when you open the drawers.

VENEERING WORK

Veneering the corner blocks

1. Make the corner blocks from frame piece cutoffs. They should mirror the corner of the face frames in dimensions.
2. Cut six matching squares of veneer a little bigger than the faces of the blocks. You want veneer to be book-matched, so start with the front faces of the front corner blocks, and reverse the veneer left and right as you go around the piece.
3. Since the veneer pieces are so small, polyvinyl acetate (PVA) or yellow glue works fine to attach them.
4. Sandwich the veneer between a caul and one side of the assembled corner block, clamp it, and let it sit to dry (see **photo B** on p. 152). Use a flat piece of plywood scrap covered with packing tape for a caul. The packing tape prevents the caul from sticking to the block.
5. When the glue is dry, trim the excess veneer around the edges with a razor knife, and then glue the other face, making sure it's lined up correctly and book-matched.

Tip: Yellow glue is normally a poor choice for veneering. Most of the problems, however, center on veneering large pieces. You can use yellow glue for very small pieces without problems, and I prefer it because it sets quickly.

Photo A: Attach the corner piece of the face frame ¾ in. shy of the bottom. This leaves a space for the corner block.

ORDER OF VENEER APPLICATION

There is a standard logic to the application of veneer as far as what surfaces to cover first. There are two factors involved: one is how it looks and the other has to do with protecting the more fragile edges. Often their relative importance has to be weighed, depending on the circumstances.

The issue is best described, I think, by imagining plastic laminate in place of the veneer. If one were to laminate the top of a counter first, then the edge, it would look terrible. That brown edge would be staring up at you all the time. And you would risk chipping the edge every time you slid something across the top. I think of the faces of the drawer fronts as the top of the counter. I veneer the top and bottom edges of each piece first, then the sides, and finally the faces.

Photo C: Glue the finished corner blocks in place. There's not much glue surface for them to attach to now, but they will be supported later by the feet.

Photo B: Pressing veneer on the small corner blocks and drawer front edges can be done easily with cauls and clamps. Apply veneer larger than the substrate surface, and trim to fit later.

6. Apply the veneer pieces to the single-piece rear blocks as well.

7. Glue and clamp the corner blocks into place. There's not a whole lot of glue area to attach these to, but they will be supported well by the feet (see **photo C**).

Veneering the drawer and side-panel edges

Veneer the edges of the drawer fronts and side panels next, using the same procedure. To size the 12mm-thick Baltic birch plywood substrate pieces, you'll need to do a little subtractive measuring.

1. For the side panels, subtract the thickness of two pieces of veneer from the overall height and width needed. The final dimensions of the side panels need to be 15⅜ in. by 5 in. So cut

panels approximately 15¼ in. by 4⅞ in. depending on the thickness of the veneer.

2. To create ³⁄₃₂-in. reveals, subtract ³⁄₃₂ in. from the height of all the drawer fronts, ³⁄₆₄ in. from the width of the side drawer fronts, and ³⁄₃₂ in. from the width of the center drawer front. These keep the parts from rubbing or jamming against one another.

3. Veneer the side edges of the panels and drawers first, then the bottom and/or top edges with PVA glue (see "Order of Veneer Application" on p. 151).

Veneering the drawer and side-panel faces

With the edges veneered, turn to the faces. Each piece is book-matched with a center seam. I use Unibond 800 (a modified urea-formaldehyde two-part adhesive, available from most veneering suppliers). Polyurethane

Photos D and E: Vacuum presses make applying veneer to the drawer fronts and side panels a cinch. Just position the pieces on the veneer in the press (left). Lower the membrane top and start the vacuum pump. The bag exerts perfectly even pressure over the parts (right).

glue also works well. I would caution against using either of these glues casually. There is a fairly high learning curve associated with them, as there is with veneering in general.

1. Glue the book-matched veneer pieces to the front of the faces and sides. I use my vacuum press, but these parts are small enough to be clamped up in the same way as the blocks and edges (see **photos D** and **E**).

2. Glue scrap veneer to the backs of the drawer fronts to avoid warping or twisting, but not to the backs of the sides (see "Bending a Veneering Rule").

3. Finish-sand the sides and drawer fronts when they're dry.

4. Attach the side panels with yellow glue and screw them down from inside the case. They should sit on top of the side frame pieces, flush with the front and top of the case and overhanging the back by ½ in.

BENDING A VENEERING RULE

A central rule in veneering is that whatever you do to one side, do to the other. Often you can use secondary (unattractive) veneer on parts that don't show, such as the backs of the drawer fronts. And I certainly don't worry about book-matching veneer on the backs and underside of things.

I broke this rule with the side panels: I veneered only their faces. As these panels will be glued directly to the plywood case, there is no chance of movement.

MAKING AND INSTALLING THE DRAWERS

Laying out the drawers

The drawers are made from 12mm-thick Baltic birch plywood (see "Baltic Birch Drawers").

1. Figure the width of the front and back of the drawer by taking the width of the opening and subtracting 1 in. for the drawer glides (most glides take up ½ in. on each side), then subtracting another 1 in. for the two ½-in. sides they fit between.

2. Calculate the lengths of the sides of the drawer by measuring the depth of the case and rounding down to the nearest drawer-glide length.

BALTIC BIRCH DRAWERS

For many years now I have been building drawers out of 12mm-thick Baltic birch plywood. It makes a nice, light, strong drawer. When well sanded and finished, even the edges are attractive without edge tape, at

least in a modern design (I wouldn't incorporate Baltic birch drawers in an 18th-century reproduction table).

I use #10 or smaller biscuits for the joinery, with 6mm Baltic birch bottoms that slide into ¼-in. dadoes

from the rear of the drawer, fastened with a few 1-in. trim-head screws. These drawers go together extremely fast. I have built hundreds of these drawers and have never had a failure.

DRAWER CONSTRUCTION

These simple and strong drawers are made from 12mm-thick Baltic birch plywood and biscuit joints. The bottom slides in from the back in a dado. The drawer front attaches to the front with four screws.

Back

Bottom

Side

Front

3⅜"

4"

13⅞"

Veneered drawer front

5"

18" (24" for center drawer)

14⅜" (21¼" for center drawer)

Milling and assembling the drawers

1. Mill the drawer parts to size.

2. Rout the groove for the bottom along the inside bottom edge of the sides and front.

3. Cut biscuit slots in the corners to join the four sides.

4. Finish-sand the inside of the drawers.

5. Glue and clamp the drawers together. When the glue is dry, sand the outside.

Attaching the drawer fronts

1. Locate the drawer fronts on the drawer boxes (see "Location and Fit of Drawers").

2. Drill the holes in the drawer box slightly oversize to allow some adjustment of the position of the drawer front.

3. Attach the drawer fronts using 1-in. wood screws and finish washers with a black finish to match the drawer glides and the black on the feet (see **photo F**).

Photo F: Screw the drawer carcase to the drawer front through holes that are slightly larger than necessary. These holes will make it possible to adjust the way the drawer front hangs when installed.

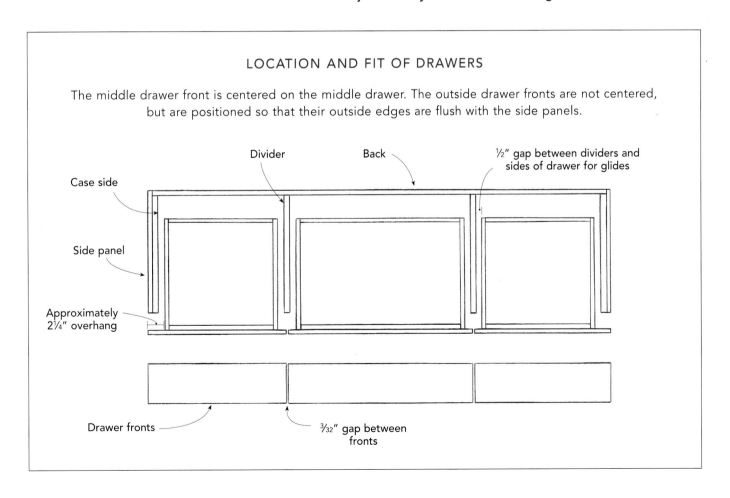

LOCATION AND FIT OF DRAWERS

The middle drawer front is centered on the middle drawer. The outside drawer fronts are not centered, but are positioned so that their outside edges are flush with the side panels.

Divider

Back

½" gap between dividers and sides of drawer for glides

Case side

Side panel

Approximately 2¼" overhang

Drawer fronts

³⁄₃₂" gap between fronts

Photo G: Slide the drawer bottom in last, and attach it with three screws at the back. It will get in the way when attaching the drawer fronts if it's put in earlier.

Photo H: Adjust the fit of the drawer front on the drawer or on the glides.

CURIOUS DIMENSIONS

If you're wondering why I had you make the front face frame ⅝ in. thick to be flush with the drawer fronts while the side frame is only ½ in., here are the details:

The drawer fronts are made from the same 12mm-thick Baltic birch plywood. Add two layers of veneer, front and back, and the thickness grows to a little less than 9/16 in.

Add the thickness of the mahogany edge tape that's applied to the raw plywood edge above the face frame and behind the drawer fronts, and you're at a little more than 9/16 in. Are you with me so far?

Add the thickness of the small bumpers you apply to the back of the drawer front to soften the sound of the drawer closing, and you're at ⅝ in., the thickness of the face frame.

4. Install the drawer bottom and check the fit (see **photo G**).

5. Separate the two parts of the drawer glide and attach the drawer part to the drawer along the centerline of the side.

6. Measure up from that line to the top of the drawer front, which will be flush with the top of the case, so you can measure down that same distance from the top of the case to find the centerline for the case part of the glide.

7. When you have both parts of the drawer glide attached, test the drawer and adjust accordingly (see **photo H**).

Cutting the Front Feet

The front feet are double tapered. Though the finished foot looks difficult to make, it takes only four simple cuts on the bandsaw to create it.

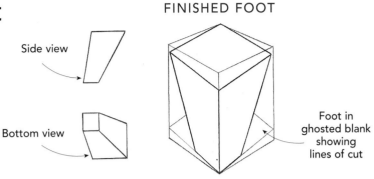

FINISHED FOOT

Side view

Bottom view

Foot in ghosted blank showing lines of cut

FIRST CUT

In a carrier that angles the workpiece 45 degrees, cut one end off the foot at a 10-degree angle.

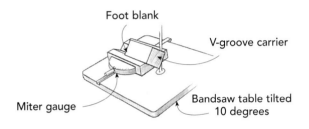

Foot blank

V-groove carrier

Miter gauge

Bandsaw table tilted 10 degrees

SECOND CUT

Cut the opposite end off the foot so it is parallel to the other.

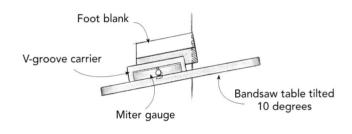

Foot blank

V-groove carrier

Miter gauge

Bandsaw table tilted 10 degrees

THIRD CUT

Freehand-cut one side of the outside taper along the layout lines.

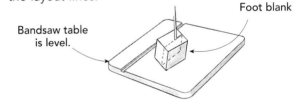

Bandsaw table is level.

Foot blank

FOURTH CUT

Freehand-cut the other side of the outside taper along the layout lines.

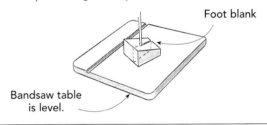

Foot blank

Bandsaw table is level.

MAKING AND ATTACHING THE FEET AND WINGS

Milling feet blanks

The smallest parts of this bookcase, the feet, are the most complicated. I find that the textured black and gold colors give the bookcase a very distinctive look. Their small size keeps them from overwhelming the rest of the piece.

The feet are constructed of two layers: blocks that support the piece and thin plywood wings attached to the surface of the blocks. The front feet are splayed 10 degrees, and their wings are mitered at the corners. The back feet aren't splayed, so the piece sits tight against the wall.

1. Glue up some 6/4 ash into four pieces approximately 5 in. long and 3 in. square, though a little thinner is fine.
2. Plane the dry feet to 2¾ in. square, and square up the ends.

Tip: Use ash for the feet because the bold grain texture telegraphs plainly through the black finish, even at a distance.

Tapering the feet

The back feet are simply tapered on the inside faces. However, the front feet are a little more complicated because they have two different tapers. The outside taper is achieved by cutting the ends of the feet at a 10-degree angle, which puts the entire leg on an angle. The inside taper is achieved by cutting a more severe taper along the inside edges (see "Cutting the Front Feet" on p. 157).

1. Cut the blanks for the two back feet 4 in. long, then measure 1⁷⁄₁₆ in. along one bottom edge and connect that mark diagonally with the top corner of the blank.

2. Cut these angles on a bandsaw.

3. Make a bandsaw carrier for cutting the ends of the front feet. It's nothing more than a block of wood a little longer than the workpiece with a 45-degree V-groove cut down the length of it, which can be done on the table saw.

4. With the carrier against the miter gauge and the piece resting in the groove, tilt your bandsaw table 10 degrees and cut one end off the piece.

5. Flip the piece end for end and cut off the other end, leaving it 4 in. long. This way, the top and bottom of the foot are parallel.

6. Level your bandsaw table.

7. Mark off 1¼ in. along the bottom edge of the foot, and then draw a line connecting that mark to the top corner of the piece.

8. Cut along that line to form the tapered inside edge of the foot.

9. Repeat the process for the last cut, making sure the right angle of the piece rests on the table.

10. Remove the bandsaw marks from all the feet with a stationary sander or whatever sander you have, then finish-sand the feet and set them aside.

Making the wings

1. Cut the wings out of 6mm Baltic birch plywood (see "Cutting the Wings for the Feet").

2. Glue the miters on the front feet together, creating two pairs. A little yellow glue and some masking tape are sufficient to hold them together as the glue dries.

3. When dry, finish-sand the wings, then glue and clamp them to their respective feet (see **photo I**). Once attached to the feet, the miter joint is well supported.

4. Cut #20 biscuit slots in the top of the back feet that will attach them to the case in the bottom edge of the frame. Don't attach the feet yet—you need to finish them first.

5. Set the jointer's fence at 10 degrees to cut the slots in the front feet.

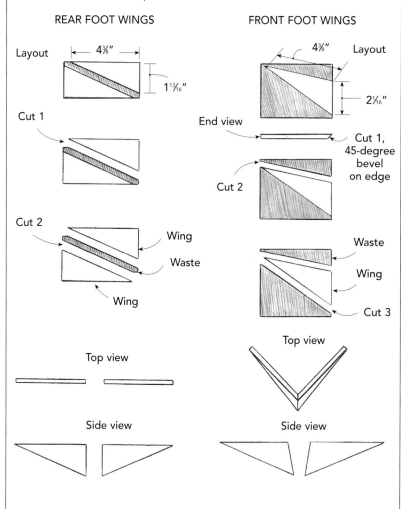

CUTTING THE WINGS FOR THE FEET

The wings for the rear feet are simple right-angle triangles. The front wings mirror the feet, being angled in two planes. You need two left-hand and two right-hand wings, so separate the blanks now into two piles and orient your cuts one way on one batch, then flip them over to cut the other batch.

REAR FOOT WINGS

Layout ├─ 4⅜" ─┤ 1¹³⁄₁₆"

Cut 1

Cut 2 Wing Waste Wing

Top view

Side view

FRONT FOOT WINGS

4⅜" Layout

End view 2¹⁄₁₆"

Cut 1, 45-degree bevel on edge

Cut 2

Waste Wing

Cut 3

Top view

Side view

Photo I: Tape, clamps, and glue are all you need to join the wings and attach them to the feet, flush with the top.

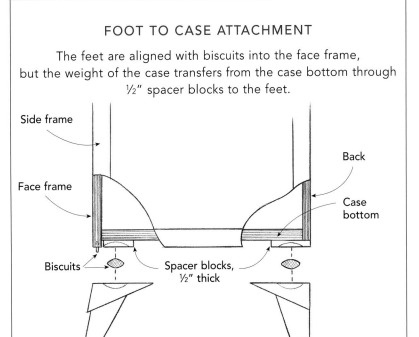

FOOT TO CASE ATTACHMENT

The feet are aligned with biscuits into the face frame, but the weight of the case transfers from the case bottom through ½" spacer blocks to the feet.

Side frame

Face frame

Biscuits

Back

Case bottom

Spacer blocks, ½" thick

Front foot

Rear foot

6. Glue a ½-in. spacer block to the tops of the feet so the bottom of the case and the sides rest directly on the feet (see "Foot to Case Attachment").

Ebonizing the feet

It's much easier to finish the feet before gluing them to the case. There are two completely different finishes on the feet that require masking and applying various materials.

1. Cover the faces of the wings with masking tape.
2. Spray the exposed surfaces on the feet with a black water-based finish called Equal (manufactured by Hydrocote; see Sources on pp. 182-183). This finish is a not very durable, but the clear coat sprayed on the whole piece at the end protects it.

Gilding the wings

I use a somewhat untraditional gilding method, but it works. If you want to learn more about gilding, there are a number of books on the subject, and some supply houses hold seminars and classes or can point you in the right direction. It is important to work in a clean space and have all your materials on hand. I find the process of gilding extremely relaxing, though I have to be methodical about it.

1. When the black is dry, I remove the tape from the faces of the wings.
2. Carefully sand the surfaces of the wings. While traditional gilding attempts to mimic a metal surface and requires that you fill the surface to make it very smooth, I prefer to have the texture of the wood telegraph through the leaf.
3. Apply two or three base coats (depending on how much the wood soaks up) of dark or Venetian Red Japan color. I use one manufactured by T. J. Ronan Paint Company. Use the best quality brush you can find and dedicate it to base-coat applications.
4. Sand between coats with 320 or 400 grit.

Tip: Gold leaf is extremely thin, almost transparent, so different-color base coats can alter the appearance of the leaf. The dark red imparts warmth to the gold. A brighter red would give it a more brash appearance.

Photo J: Gilding the wings involves the use of several brushes, Japan color, size varnish, and gold leaf. Nevertheless, it is no more difficult than most other finishing processes.

Tip: Be careful to keep the glue in the biscuit slots. You don't want any squeeze-out, especially along the front edges, since there is no way to clean it off the gold without taking the gold off, too.

5. When the last base coat is good and dry, apply one fairly thin, even coat of size. The size coat is a varnish that does the double duty of sealing the base coat and acting as the adhesive for the gold leaf. I use Rolco Quick-Dry Synthetic Gold Size Varnish (see Sources on pp. 182-183).

6. Let the varnish dry for about a half hour, then apply the gold leaf (see "When to Apply the Gold Leaf to the Size Coat").

7. Transfer the gold leaf from the book to the workpiece with a very fine, wide brush called a gilder's tip (see **photo J**). Pick up the leaf with the brush, float it over to the wing (gold leaf is very thin), and then lightly lay it on.

8. Continue this process, overlapping the sheets, until the entire surface is covered. Overlapped sheets will not show a seam because the leaf is so thin.

9. Use an extremely soft brush called a gilder's mop to smooth the leaf and remove all the loose leaf.

Attaching the feet

The feet are attached to the bottom frame with biscuits, but the weight of the piece rests on the $\frac{1}{2}$-in. spacer blocks attached to the top of each foot.

Spread glue only into the biscuit slot and the center of the spacer block and clamp each foot in place (see **photo K**).

ATTACHING THE TOP AND FINISHING

Making and attaching the subtop

The granite top needs a slightly smaller ¾-in.-thick subtop to make it float visually. The subtop is recessed ¾ in. on each side and in the front, and flush in the back. It's also gilded around the front and side edges. I would not normally gild a plywood edge, but I needed to use plywood rather than a solid wood frame because full support was required under the granite top.

1. Fill the edge of the subtop plywood with auto-body filler to make it smooth.
2. Gild the plywood edge.
3. Screw the subtop in place on top of the case.

Finishing

You should finish the piece now with whatever finish you prefer. I finished my bookcase with a clear water-based finish called Resisthane manufactured and distributed by Hood Finishing Products, Inc. (see Sources on pp. 182-183). Hydrocote also manufactures the black finish I used earlier on the feet. I prefer to leave gilded surfaces without any finish. But for surfaces that will become worn, such as these feet, it's best to apply a clear top coat, which, again, will be taken care of when I finish the whole piece.

Adding the black granite top

There is no need to adhere or fasten the granite: Its weight is more than sufficient to keep it in place. The granite I used is called Absolute Black. It comes ¾ in. thick and should be available from any granite, marble, or stone supplier.

1. Make a ¼-in. plywood template the exact size of the stone and give it to a granite supplier. Make sure you emphasize that it needs to be exactly the size of the template after the edges are polished.
2. Simply place the granite top on the finished piece. By the way, this is a job for more than one person.

Tip: If you normally sand between coats of finish, you will almost certainly ruin the gold leaf. Let the finish build up between coats without sanding on the gilded parts, and sand only between the last two coats.

STEP-BACK BOOKCASE

The Step-Back Bookcase is extremely versatile and, consequently, very popular. I build a fair number of them for my clients and see this type of bookcase in living rooms more often than almost any other kind. It incorporates the best features of a wall unit or entertainment center, without the bulk.

There is a fair amount of enclosed space in the base to stash things that you'd like to keep handy but not necessarily display. Add to this a large amount of display space in the upper section and a deep counter for everything from large bowls or vases to family photos. This design is also easily adapted to reflect almost any popular style, from Shaker to Arts and Crafts. And because it knocks down into two pieces, it is relatively easy to move. For all these reasons and more, you can see why this type of case is so popular.

This particular step-back bookcase is one of a pair I built. They flank a large couch in a fairly formal living room, so along with storage and display, they also serve as end tables. They are identical except for the internals of the base sections. One has three adjustable shelves, and the other (the one featured here) has just one adjustable shelf but is also outfitted to hold a stereo and has a drawer for CDs.

Step-Back Bookcase

THE STEP-BACK BOOKCASE KNOCKS DOWN into a lower and upper case to make it easy to move. It has fixed shelves in the upper case. The lower case has a drawer hidden by doors and two shelves, one adjustable. The carcases are made of ¾-in. plywood joined with biscuits. Solid-wood edging is attached where the plywood edges would show. The top face frame piece doubles as the front piece of crown molding. Black trim accents and quilted moabie veneer on the door panels give the piece depth.

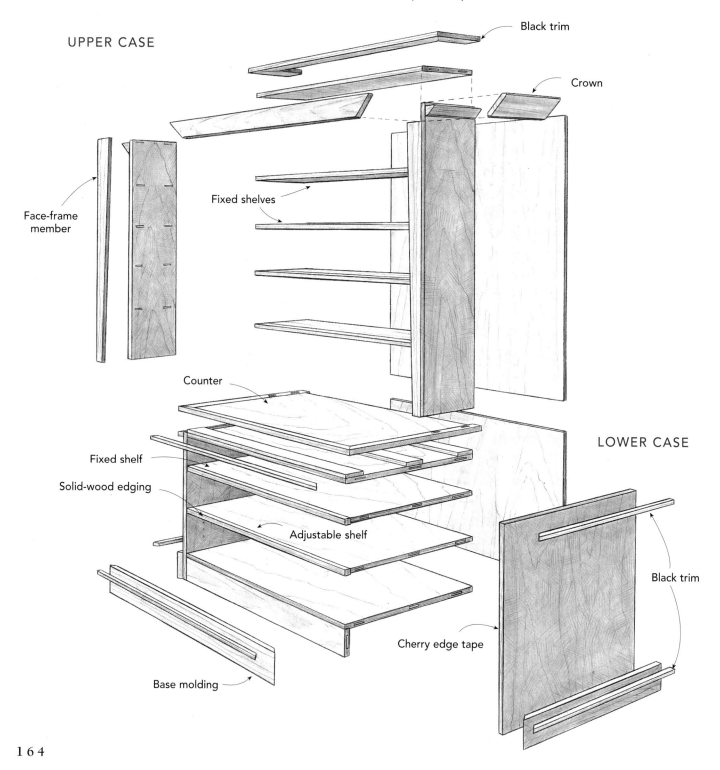

UPPER CASE

Black trim

Crown

Fixed shelves

Face-frame member

Counter

Fixed shelf

Solid-wood edging

Adjustable shelf

LOWER CASE

Black trim

Cherry edge tape

Base molding

FRONT VIEW

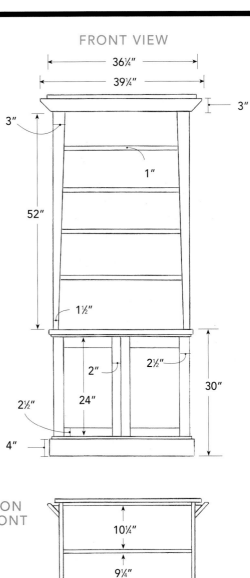

36¼"

39¼"

3"

3"

1"

52"

1½"

2"

2½"

24"

2½"

4"

30"

SIDE VIEW

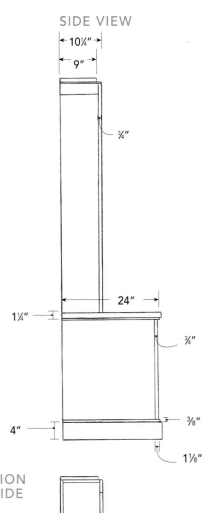

10¼"

9"

¾"

24"

1¼"

¾"

4"

⅜"

1⅛"

SECTION OF FRONT

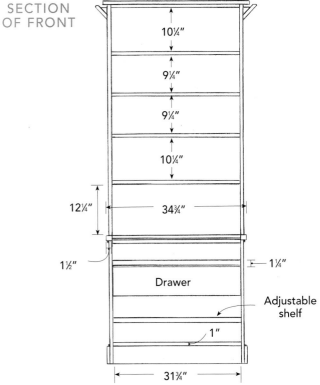

10¼"

9¼"

9¼"

10¼"

12¼"

34¾"

1½"

1¼"

Drawer

Adjustable shelf

1"

31¾"

SECTION OF SIDE

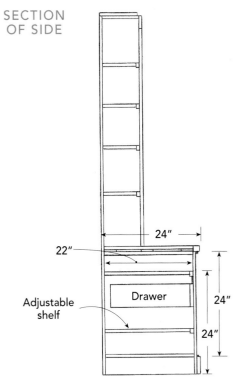

24"

22"

Drawer

Adjustable shelf

24"

24"

BUILDING THE BOOKCASE STEP-BY-STEP

CUT LIST FOR STEP-BACK BOOKCASE

Upper Case

2	Sides	55 in. x 9½ in. x ¾ in., cherry plywood
1	Top	31¾ in. x 9 in. x ¾ in., cherry plywood
4	Shelves	31¾ in. x 8¼ in. x ¾ in., cherry plywood
1	Back	56¼ in. x 32½ in. x ½ in., cherry plywood
2	Face frame stiles	52 in. x 3 in. x ¾ in., solid cherry
1	Crown piece	39¼ in. x 3 in. x ¾ in., solid cherry
2	Crown pieces	9½ in. x 3¼ in. x ¾ in., solid cherry
2	Backup pieces for crown	9½ in. x 1¹¹⁄₁₆ in. x 1¹¹⁄₁₆ in., solid cherry
4	Edging for top shelves	31¾ in. x 1 in. x ¾ in., solid cherry

Lower Case

1	Top	31¾ in. x 22 in. x ¾ in., cherry plywood
1	Subtop	31¾ in. x 22 in. x ¾ in., cherry plywood
2	Sides	28¾ in. x 22½ in. x ¾ in., cherry plywood
1	Bottom	31¾ in. x 22 in. x ¾ in., cherry plywood
2	Shelves	31¾ in. x 21¼ in. x ¾ in., cherry plywood
1	Kick	31¾ in. x 4 in. x ¾ in., cherry plywood
1	Back	28¼ in. x 32½ in. x ½ in., cherry plywood
1	Base molding piece	34¾ in. x 4 in. x ¾ in., solid cherry
2	Base molding pieces	24 in. x 4 in. x ¾ in., solid cherry
1	Backup for base molding	33¼ in. x 4 in. x ¾ in., solid cherry
2	Edging for top of lower case	24 in. x 1½ in. x 1¼ in., solid cherry
1	Edging for top of lower case	34¾ in. x 1½ in. x 1¼ in., solid cherry
1	Edging for lower shelves	31¾ in. x 1¼ in. x ¾ in., solid cherry
1	Edging for lower shelves	31¾ in. x 1 in. x ¾ in., solid cherry

THE CONSTRUCTION of this bookcase is similar to the sideboard bookcase on pp. 144–161. Both are essentially plywood boxes joined with biscuits, use veneers, and have face frames. After the upper and lower cases are assembled, various elements are added to create the style. The use of a decorative veneer on the panels is a very simple way to dress up a door, and coloring the accent trim black distinguishes otherwise austere moldings.

MAKING THE UPPER AND LOWER CASES

Sizing the plywood and milling the solid wood parts

So much of this bookcase is made with cherry plywood that you should size every piece at the same time. This approach will reduce the total time you spend on the project (you don't have to set up machines for the same cuts twice) and reduce waste because you can plan the use of each sheet (as I did for the bookcase on pp. 32–45). It's a more complicated process, however, because you're juggling many more parts in your head (and in your shop) at once. Do the same with the solid wood parts as well.

1. Make a good working drawing of the bookcase to orient yourself and a well-thought-out cut list to keep track of the pieces.
2. Lay out and size all the plywood to make the cores of the upper and lower cases (see "Plywood Case Construction" on p. 168).
3. Mark each part's location and orientation.
4. On the inside rear edge of each case side, cut a ½-in.-wide by ⅜-in.-deep rabbet. This rabbet will house the ½-in. plywood backs.
5. Lay out and cut all the biscuit slots for the upper and lower cases.
6. Lay out and size all the solid wood pieces.

Applying edge treatments to the shelving

The four fixed shelves in the upper section and the single fixed shelf in the lower case get solid wood edging.

1. Attach the edging to the fronts of all the fixed shelves, using biscuits to keep the top of the plywood and the edging flush (see **photo A** on p. 169).

2. Cut all the fixed shelves to finished size, then sand the top edges flush.

3. Cover the front edges of the top, bottom, and sides of the lower case with iron-on cherry edge tape.

4. Trim and sand the tape flush with all the edges.

Drilling shelf pin holes in the lower case sides

The lower case has an adjustable shelf. You need to drill a series of shelf pin holes for it in the area that will be below the fixed shelf and the CD drawer.

1. Lay out the 10 holes on both sides carefully, 1 in. apart and approximately 2 in. from the front and back.

2. Drill the holes by hand. If you worry that your shelf might rock from misaligned holes, you can use a line-boring jig as described on pp. 41-42.

3. Finish-sand the top, bottom, and front faces of all the shelves and the insides of the case pieces to 180 grit while they are apart and easily accessible.

Gluing up the cases

1. Lay one side, inside face up, on your bench and glue in the biscuits.

2. Apply glue into the biscuit slots and down the center between the slots on one end of the shelves and the top.

3. One by one, position the pieces on the biscuits. Both the shelves and the top should be flush with the front edge and the inside of the rabbet in the rear of the sides.

CUT LIST FOR STEP-BACK BOOKCASE

Doors

2	Stiles	24 in. x 2½ in. x ¾ in., solid cherry
2	Stiles	24 in. x 2 in. x ¾ in., solid cherry
4	Rails	14⅞ in. x 2½ in. x ¾ in., solid cherry
2	Door panels	9¾ in. x 12⅞ in. x 6mm, 5-ply Baltic birch plywood

Drawers

1	Drawer part	31½ in. x 7 in. x ¾ in., solid cherry
1	Drawer part	26⅝ in. x 5⅜ in. x ¾ in., solid cherry
2	Drawer parts	19¾ in. x 5⅜ in. x ¾ in., solid cherry
2	Drawer parts	26⅝ in. x 4¾ in. x ½ in., solid cherry
1	Drawer bottom	27⅜ in. x 20½ in. x 6mm, 5-ply Baltic birch plywood
12	Drawer dividers	6¼ in. x 4¾ in. x 6mm, 5-ply Baltic birch plywood

Black Trim

1	Top trim	36¼ in. x 2 in. x 1 in., solid cherry
2	Top trim	9 in. x 2 in. x 1 in., solid cherry
4	Bottom trim	23⅝ in. x ⅜ in. x ⅜ in., solid cherry
2	Bottom trim	34 in. x 1⅛ in. x ⅜ in., solid cherry

Miscellaneous

15 sq. ft.	quilted moabie veneer
15 lin. ft.	cherry iron-on edge tape
4	Shelf pins
4	European-style hinges
4	Pair knockdown fasteners
2	Decorative pulls

Tip: Leave the shelves slightly wider and longer than finished size. This allows for more precise sizing by ripping and crosscutting them to size after their edges are glued on.

Plywood Case Construction

The cases are assembled from pieces of plywood. Use these drawings to connect each correctly.

UPPER CASE

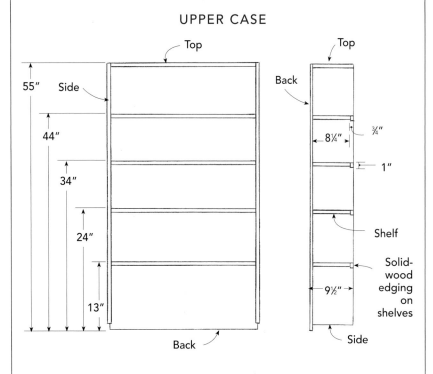

LOWER CASE

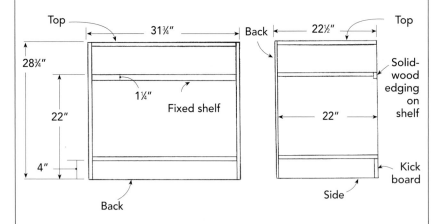

4. Glue the other side and clamp the case across the front and back of each shelf and the top. The lower case is assembled the same way, except the shelf is recessed ⅛ in. from the front edge of the sides and flush with the inside edge of the rabbet.

DRESSING UP THE UPPER CASE

Making a face frame and crown molding

The traditional treatment for the upper case of a step-back bookcase is a three-piece face frame (a top and two sides) and a three-piece crown molding around the top. I integrated the face frame and crown molding where they intersect so the top piece of the face frame is also the front piece of the crown molding. The detail is interesting and subtle, and fewer parts mean the construction is simpler (see "Crown Detail").

1. Cut the 3-in. by ¾-in. piece for the front crown (that you milled earlier) square on the ends and a little long.

2. Mark a vertical centerline on the top edge of this piece and the top of the case.

3. Starting from this line, lay out for biscuit slots to the left and right out to the ends.

4. Cut these slots and temporarily clamp this piece in place, lining up the centerlines. The centerlines allow you to return it to exactly the same place on the carcase later.

5. Mark the line of taper on the side frame pieces along the inside edges from 3 in. at the top to 1½ in. at the bottom.

6. Carefully cut close to the line on a band-saw (a jigsaw will work just as well, though not as fast).

7. Clean up the cut edge by running it across a jointer, taking several light cuts until you reach the line. The tapers do not need to be exactly perfect or exactly the same. If they look fine, then they are fine.

8. Lay out and cut the biscuit slots that will connect these members flush with the sides of the case. Temporarily clamp them in place.

Crown Detail

The front crown lies flat against the case but intersects the crown molding on the sides, which are angled.

SIDE VIEW

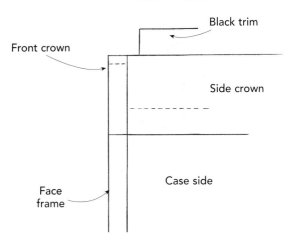

FRONT VIEW

With top front face frame member removed.

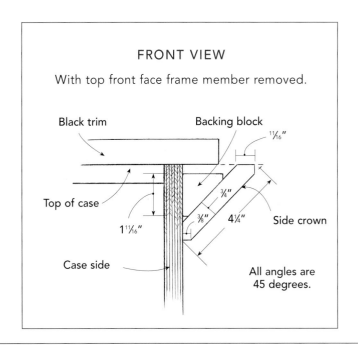

All angles are 45 degrees.

Photo A: Solid-wood edging is attached to the front edges of the plywood shelves.

Tip: Don't attach the backs yet. They go on near the end of the work. Leaving them off for now makes clamping a large number of pieces much easier.

9. With both the sides and top of the face frame clamped in place, mark for two more biscuit slots where the tops of the side pieces butt against the top piece (see **photo B**), but don't cut them yet.

Attaching the face frame and crown returns

With the face-frame parts clamped in place, turn to the side crown returns. These are two pieces of crown molding on the sides of the case that are biscuited into the face frame.

1. Mill the profile of these pieces on the table saw and cut one end square (see "Crown Detail" on p. 169).

2. Hold them in place against the back of the top frame piece and mark their shape where they intersect the front piece.

3. Now remove the top face frame member and, using these marks, cut the ends to match the crown returns.

4. Reinstall the top face frame member and check the fit against the returns.

5. Once you're satisfied with the fit, mark for a biscuit slot where they meet. Do this for both returns.

6. Remove the entire face frame and cut the biscuit slots that join the top face frame member to the side pieces and the crown returns.

7. Sand the inside faces and edges of the face frame and glue, biscuit, and clamp them in place. These pieces are done and don't need to be removed again.

8. Find and mark the location of the backing blocks by dry-fitting biscuits into the crown return pieces, positioning them level and even with the front, then by fitting the backing blocks behind them.

9. Screw the backing blocks in place from the inside of the case. These screws are high up and behind the upper frame member, so they won't be seen.

10. Permanently fasten the crown returns with glue in the biscuit joint and along the backing block. Clamping them in place until the glue dries (see **photo C**).

Photo B: Dry-clamp the three pieces of face frame on the upper case to mark for the biscuit joints that will join them.

Tip: It's extremely important that the ends of the top face frame piece be cut and shaped exactly right, otherwise the side returns that make up the rest of the crown will never fit.

Photo C: The crown molding returns are biscuited into the front face frame piece and glued to the backing blocks.

Photo D: Simply glue the three baseboards in place. Add a backing block in front so the base stands proud of the doors the same distance the side pieces stand proud of the sides.

COMPLETING THE LOWER CASE

Attaching the base molding

1. Finish-sand the outside of the case.

2. Attach a ¾-in. by 4-in.-wide backup board to the front of the case where the base molding will be. Because the doors on this section are overlay doors, the front base has to be blocked forward by ¾ in. so that the base has the same reveal in the front as it does on the sides.

3. Miter the base molding pieces at the corners where they intersect.

4. Glue and clamp the three pieces of base in place (see **photo D**).

5. Once the glue is dry, finish-sand the molding and set the case aside.

Attaching the base top

The lower case has a countertop consisting of a piece of ¾-in. cherry plywood, edged with 1½-in. by 1¼-in. solid cherry that is mitered at the front corners.

1. Fit all three solid cherry pieces on the countertop, making sure the front piece is the precise length and won't leave a gap at each corner.

2. Miter, biscuit, glue, and clamp the front edging in place.

Photo E: Clamp up one side of the mitered edging to the top at a time. To make sure the corners are tight, put one clamp between the end of the side piece and the front corner.

3. Miter the sides and cut them to length. The side edging should extend ½ in. past the back edge of the top to accommodate the back.

4. Before attaching the side edging, cut a ½-in. by ¾-in. notch on the inside back edges of these pieces, also to accommodate the back.

5. Biscuit, glue, and clamp the side edging in place (see **photo E**).

6. Cut three 3-in. strips of ½-in. plywood and glue and screw them flat on top of the lower case, front, back, and center. Be sure to align them ¾ in. in from each side. This plywood fills the ½-in. space between the underside of the top and the top of the case, supporting the weight of the upper section.

7. Finish-sand and firmly screw the top in place from the inside through these strips onto the lower case.

8. Make and install the drawer for the CDs. It's very similar in construction and identical in installation to the drawers in the Formal Sideboard Bookcase (also see "A CD Drawer").

A CD DRAWER

The drawer on this bookcase is designed specifically to hold CDs (compact discs, not certificates of deposit), so they are easily organized and accessible.

I devised a system of dividers to organize the CDs. The long dividers fit into the drawer sides with biscuits. The short dividers slide down into the long dividers and are movable. The dividers are 4¾ in. deep, making it easy to pick out a CD, which is 5⁵⁄₁₆ in. tall on end. I also cut a step in the top edge of the front to allow the front dividers to be installed and removed (see the photo on the facing page).

The 6mm Baltic birch plywood I used has edges decorative enough not to be covered. You can see for yourself what this plywood looks like in the photo, and if you don't like the effect, use solid wood.

Because multiples of the width of a CD plus the divider widths did not add up to a number that could be divided evenly in the space available, I made the drawer a little smaller and added spacers to hold the drawer glides and fill the space.

Otherwise this drawer is similar in construction to the drawers for the Formal Sideboard Bookcase on pp. 154-156, but there are several notable differences. The drawer sides, front, and back are solid stock, not plywood. The drawer front is integral, not added on. Since the drawer front extends past the sides of the drawer to cover the drawer glides, the biscuits that connect the edges are inset.

CONSTRUCTION OF DRAWER AND LAYOUT OF DIVIDERS

TOP VIEW

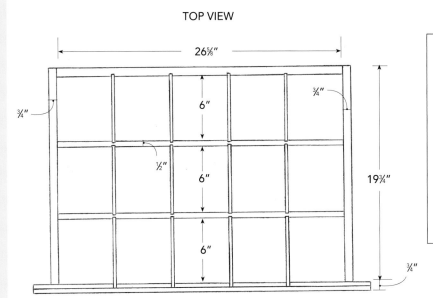

SIDE VIEW

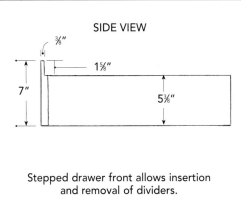

Stepped drawer front allows insertion and removal of dividers.

FRONT VIEW (CROSS SECTION)

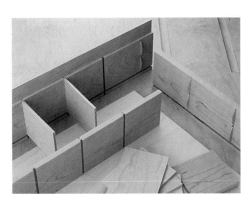

The drawer is divided into compartments to hold CDs. The sides and long dividers are connected with biscuits. The short plywood dividers can be removed.

Photo F: The Simplex interlocking wafers, manufactured by Lamello, turn a biscuit joint into a knockdown joint.

COMPLETING AND CONNECTING THE CASES

Attaching the backs

The backs for the upper and lower cases are both ½-in. cherry plywood.

1. Cut the backs to size. The back for the lower section extends from the floor to the top of the case, or 1¼ in. down from the countertop. The back for the top section extends 1¼ in. below the bottom of the upper sides so it butts against the lower back.
2. Check the fit of both backs, but install only the lower back for now.

Making the knockdown joint that connects the cases

The top and bottom cases have to be connected with a knockdown joint, or the upper case would be very unstable and easily dislodged from its base. I use a very simple variation on a biscuit joint: Simplex knockdown fasteners manufactured by Lamello (see Sources on pp. 182-183). They fit into the normal slots cut by a biscuit joiner (see **photo F**).

1. Cut two biscuit slots in the countertop and in the bottom of the top case sides, registering the fence off the outside face.
2. Position the upper section carefully on top of the base, marking where the sides sit.
3. Remove the upper section and clamp a piece of scrap along these lines for a fence to register the biscuit joiner.
4. Cut the mating slots in the countertop.
5. Insert the Simplex wafers into the biscuit slots with a small amount of epoxy and allow it to cure (about 12 hours).
6. Carefully position the top case onto the fasteners and slide the two halves of the fasteners together, being careful not to scratch the top of the lower case.
7. Install the upper back in the case and insert some screws through it into the back edge of the top of the base section, locking the two sections together (see "Simplex Knockdown Joint").

Ebonizing and attaching the trim

This piece has a number of ebonized decorative trim pieces—above the crown, under the lower case top, and above the base of the lower case. The side pieces of trim under the top and above the base of the lower section are ⅜ in. square and are simply mitered at the front edge. The front pieces are attached under and on top of the doors. They add ¾ in. to the total height of the doors.

Simplex Knockdown Joint

The upper and lower cases are joined with Simplex aluminum knockdown fasteners in the upper case sides and the lower case countertop. They fit into normal biscuit slots. The cases are also secured with a few screws to keep the piece from being knocked apart by accident.

SIDE SECTION VIEW

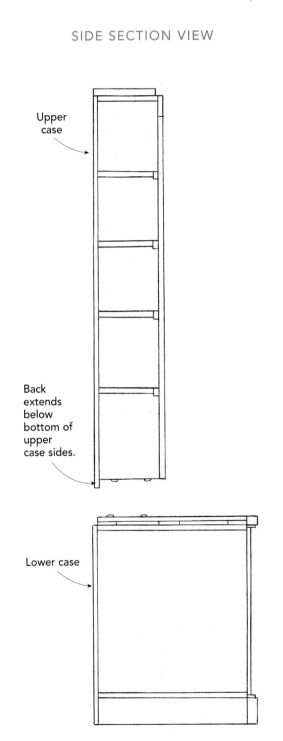

Upper case

Back extends below bottom of upper case sides.

Lower case

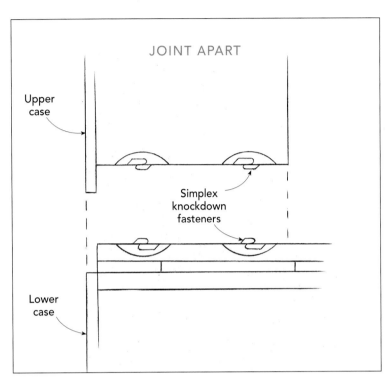

JOINT APART

Upper case

Simplex knockdown fasteners

Lower case

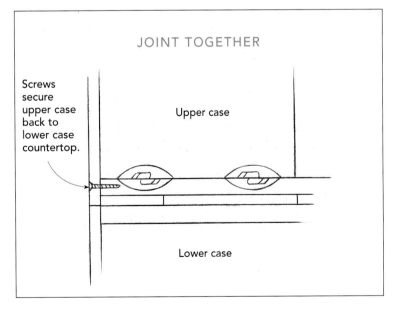

JOINT TOGETHER

Screws secure upper case back to lower case countertop.

Upper case

Lower case

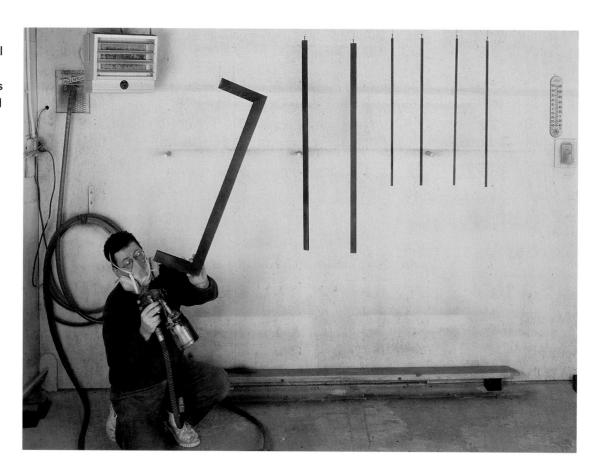

Photo G: For a deep black finish, spray all the trim parts with black lacquer, such as Equal, a water-based finish manufactured by Hydrocote.

LOWER CASE BLACK TRIM MITER

In order for the front trim pieces to extend past the face of the doors the same ⅜″ as the sides, they are 1⅛″ wide (the thickness of the door is ¾″ added to the ⅜″ extension). Miter these into the side pieces as shown.

PLAN VIEW

Side trim

⅜″

Side trim

Location of door when closed

Front trim

1⅛″

⅜″ reveal

Front trim

⅜″ reveal

Photo H: Veneer both sides of the door panels and clamp them together in a vacuum or other type of veneer press.

1. Cut all the trim pieces to size.

2. For the trim above the crown, miter together three 2-in. by 1-in. pieces of solid stock, creating a U-shaped assembly 9 in. deep and 36¼ in. wide.

3. Finish all the trim pieces and the U-shaped assembly in the same manner as for the feet on the Formal Sideboard Bookcase (see p. 159 and **photo G**).

4. Screw the U-shaped assembly to the top of the upper case.

5. Miter and install the bottom case trim after the stock is finished. So that the connections are essentially unseen, use very small brads with their heads cut off or shoot headless pins about the diameter of a straight pin with an air nailer (see "Lower Case Black Trim Miter").

6. Blacken the unfinished cut miters on the bottom case trim with a black felt marker before butting together. Believe me, it works just fine.

MAKING AND INSTALLING THE DOORS

Veneering the door panels

The veneered panels for the doors will take some time to dry after being assembled, so apply the quilted moabie veneer to the front and back of the two door panels before starting the door frames. I use a vacuum veneer press (see **photo H**). For more details on the veneering process, see either pp. 151-153 or *The Veneering Book* by David Shath Square (The Taunton Press, 1995).

Tip: If veneering is beyond your current ability or desire, the bookcase looks great with figured solid wood cherry panels or anything else that suits your taste.

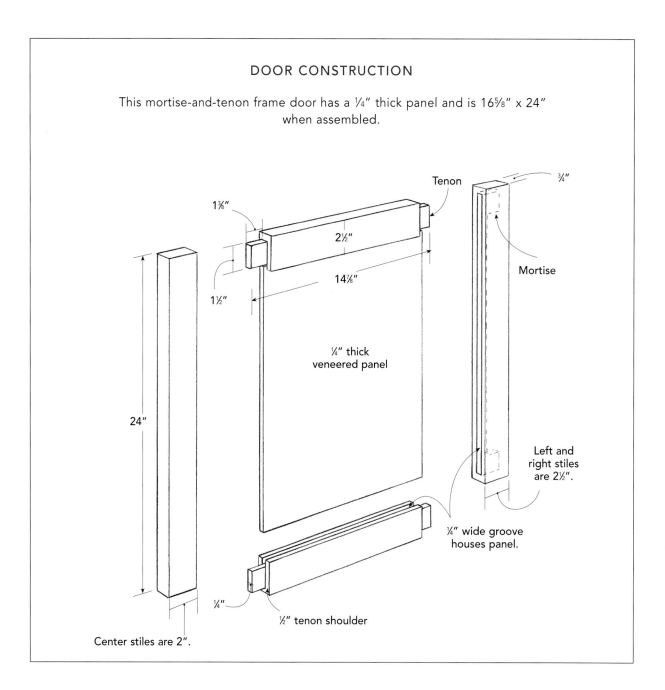

DOOR CONSTRUCTION

This mortise-and-tenon frame door has a ¼" thick panel and is 16⅝" x 24" when assembled.

Tenon

1⅜"

2½"

¾"

Mortise

14⅞"

1½"

¼" thick
veneered panel

24"

Left and
right stiles
are 2½".

¼" wide groove
houses panel.

¼"

½" tenon shoulder

Center stiles are 2".

Making and assembling the doors

1. If you haven't already done so, mill the door frame parts to size.

2. Cut ¼-in.-wide centered mortises 1⅜ in. deep at both ends of all the stiles.

3. Chuck a ¼-in. straight bit into a router table and set the fence to cut a ¼-in.-wide by ⅜-in.-deep groove centered on the rails and stiles.

4. Cut the grooves between the mortises on each end. Carefully lower the workpiece onto the router bit inside the first mortise, run the workpiece along the router bit until it enters the next mortise, and carefully lift the work-piece off.

5. Use the same setup to cut the panel grooves in the rails. In this case, there is no need to start and stop the groove because the rails have no end grain that shows when the

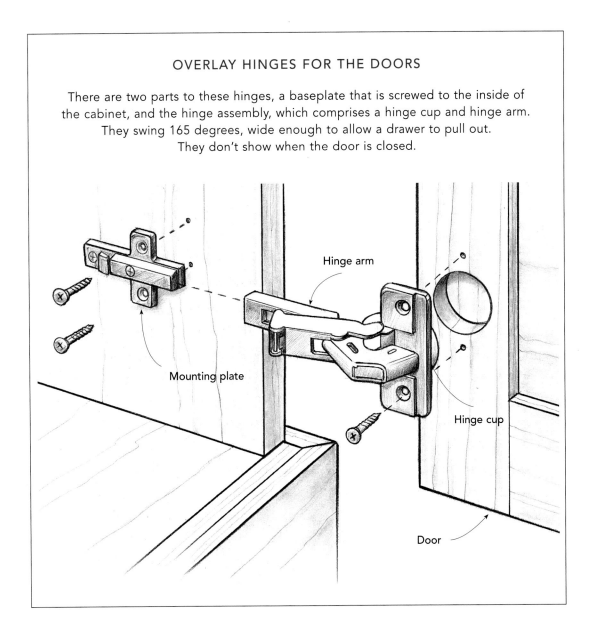

OVERLAY HINGES FOR THE DOORS

There are two parts to these hinges, a baseplate that is screwed to the inside of the cabinet, and the hinge assembly, which comprises a hinge cup and hinge arm. They swing 165 degrees, wide enough to allow a drawer to pull out. They don't show when the door is closed.

Hinge arm

Mounting plate

Hinge cup

Door

doors are assembled. Just run the groove through from one end to the other (see "Door Construction").

6. Cut the tenons on the table saw, as for the Barrister Bookcase doors on pp. 132-143. For these doors, however, you make an extra cut on the outside edges of the rails since the tenon is not the full width of the rails.

7. Trim the panels to size, and finish-sand them and the inside edges of the door frames.

8. Spread some glue into the mortises, and assemble and clamp the doors.

9. When the doors are dry, sand all the faces flush, then finish-sand them.

Installing the doors

These doors are hung on European hinges, which are also called concealed hinges. I chose these hinges for several reasons. First, they contribute to an uncluttered contemporary look because they can't be seen when the doors are closed. Second, they make hanging the doors easy because they're adjustable. Third, and perhaps most important to this bookcase, they are one of only a few types of hinges available that allow a door to swing out and away from the case far enough for a full-width drawer to be pulled out (see "Overlay Hinges for the Doors").

Photo I: Drill the hinge cup hole in the door stile on a drill press to ensure that the hole is not skewed.

1. Locate the center of the hinge cup hole on the back side of the door.

2. Measure in from the edge of the door 22.5mm (⅞ in.) and up from the bottom and down from the top somewhere between 2½ in. and 3½ in.

3. Drill a 35mm (1⅜ in.) hole 13mm (½ in.) deep at this location (see **photo I**).

4. Insert the hinge cup into the hole, and position the hinge arm perpendicular to the edge of the door. Screw the cup in place (see **photo J**).

5. Locate the mounting plate on the inside of the cabinet so the center of the two front holes is 36mm (1¹³⁄₃₂ in.) from the front edge of the cabinet and positioned an appropriate distance up or down to line up with the hinge arm (see **photo K**).

6. Attach the hinge arm to the mounting plate, and your door is hung, plain and simple.

7. Fine-tune the way the doors hang by means of the internal adjustments in the hinge. The hinges have a range of ¹⁄₁₆ in. in and out, side to side, and up and down.

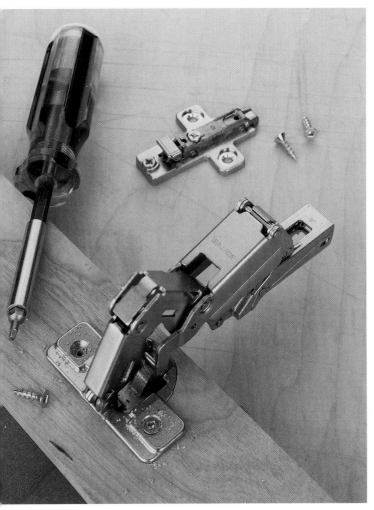

Photo J: Make sure that the hinge arm is perpendicular to the stile when you attach it with screws.

Photo K: Install the mounting plate on the inside face of the cabinet side.

FINISHING

Staining the cabinet darker

Though the cherry is beautiful left in its natural color, the people I built this bookcase for wanted it darker and more brown. I experimented with several brands, types, and colors of stain, and I finally used Minwax walnut. A warning about this stain: When first applied, it gives cherry a decidedly green tint, but it changes overnight to a more mellow color and darkens after a few months to what you see in the photo on p. 162.

For the top coat, I applied a clear water-based finish called Resisthane manufactured by Hydrocote and distributed by Hood Finishing Products, Inc. (see Sources on pp. 182-183). Cherry is notorious for blotching when stained, but I find this to be a problem mostly with solid cherry. Veneered cherry accepts stain much better, and dark stains are even less of a problem. I'm also not so disturbed by this phenomenon as a lot of people are, as I find it tends to even out over time.

SOURCES

BAGGOT LEAF CO.
430 Broome St.
New York, NY 10013-3260
(212) 431-4653
Gold leaf and gilding supplies

CERTAINLY WOOD
13000 Route 78
East Aurora, NY 14052-9515
(716) 655-0206
Veneers

CONSTANTINE'S
2050 Eastchester Rd.
Bronx, NY 10461
(800) 223-8087
Veneer, veneering supplies, and wood-working supplies

CRAFTSMAN HARDWARE CO.
P.O. Box 161
Maraline, MO 64658
(660) 376-2481
Hand-crafted and custom Arts and Crafts hardware

CROWN CITY HARDWARE
1047 N. Allen Ave.
Pasadena, CA 91104
(818) 794-1188
Antique reproduction hardware

EASY LEAF
6001 Santa Monica Blvd.
Los Angeles, CA 90038
(213) 469-0856
Gold leaf and gilding supplies

ECO DESIGN CO.
The Natural Choice
1365 Rufina Circle
Santa Fe, NM 87505
(800) 621-2591
Bioshield finishes and paints for the environment

ECOTIMBER
1020 Heinz Ave.
Berkeley, CA 94710
(510) 549-3000
ecotimber@ecotimber.com
Specialty lumber

EQUALITY SCREW
1815 John Towers Ave.
P.O. Box 1645
El Cajon, CA 92022-1645
(800) 854-2886
Cabinet screws and drivers

GARRETT WADE
161 Ave. of the Americas
New York, NY 10013
(800) 221-2942
Sutherland Welles polymerized tung oil, Hot Stuff Super 'T' CA (cyanoacrylate adhesive), and specialty woodworking tools and supplies

HIGHLAND HARDWARE
1045 N. Highland Ave. NE
Atlanta, GA 30306
(800) 241-6748
Hydrocote water-based finishes, tools, and woodworking supplies

HOOD FINISHING PRODUCTS, INC.
P.O. Box 220
Tennent, NJ 08873
(800) 229-0934
Hydrocote water-based finishes, including Equal and Resisthane

LARRY & FAYE BRUSSO CO.
4865 Highland Rd., Suite J
Waterford, MI 48328
(248) 674-8458
Knife hinges, bullet catches, and other specialty brass hardware

LEE VALLEY TOOLS LTD.
P.O. Box 1780
Ogdensburg, NY 13669-9973
(800) 871-8158
Veritas line-boring jig, CCKL Creator protractor gauge, polyurethane glue, hardware, tools, and woodworking supplies

McFEELY'S
1620 Wythe Rd.
Lynchburg, VA 24506-1169
(800) 443-7937
Square drive screws, fasteners, drill bits, tools, and woodworking supplies

M. L. CONDON CO. INC.
South Greenhaven Rd.
Stormville, NY 12582
(914) 221-8966
Ebony and other specialty woods

OLD FASHIONED MILK PAINT CO.
P.O. Box 222
Groton, MA 01450
(978) 448-6336
Milk paint and antique crackle

OUTWATER HARDWARE
11 West End Rd.
Totowa, NJ 07512
(800) 631-0342
*Euro screws, Accuride drawer glides,
European concealed hinges, hardware,
and tools*

ROCKLER
4365 Willow Dr.
Medina, MN 55340
(800) 279-4441
*Jig It line-boring jig, Accuride drawer
glides, European concealed hinges, hardware, tools, and woodworking supplies*

SALICE AMERICA
2123 Crow Center Dr.
Charlotte, NC 28227
(800) 222-9652
*European concealed hinges and func-
tional hardware*

SELECT MACHINERY INC.
64-30 Ellwell Crescent
Rego Park, NY 11374
(718) 897-3937
*Lamello Simplex fasteners, Lamello
machines and accessories*

STAFAST PRODUCTS INC.
2426 W. Highway 160
Ft. Mill, SC 29715
(803) 548-1542
*Connector bolts, Euro screws, and
assorted fasteners*

TOOLGUIDE CORP.
2533 N. Carson St., Suite 3063
Carson City, NV 89706
(888) 463-3786
*Festo Tools: FS-LR 32 hole-drilling
system and other Festo power tools*

VACUUM PRESSING SYSTEMS INC.
553 River Rd.
Brunswick, MA 04011
(207) 725-0935
vps@vupress.com
*Vacuum veneer presses, Unibond 800
glue, veneering supplies, and honeycomb
cores*

VAN DYKES RESTORERS
P.O. Box 278
Woonsocket, SD 57385
(800) 558-1234
*Reproduction fine-finish cut nails, repro-
duction and restoration hardware and
accessories*

WHITECHAPEL LTD.
P.O. Box 136
Wilson, WY 83014
(800) 468-5534
*Reproduction period hardware, cut nails,
Tried and True varnish oil, antiquing
solution*

WHITESIDE MACHINE &
REPAIR CO. INC.
4506 Shook Rd.
Claremont, NC 25610
(800) 225-3982
Router bits and assorted cutters

WOODCRAFT
120 Wood Country Industrial Park
P.O. Box 1686
Parkersburg, WV 26102-1686
(800) 225-1153
*Specialty woods, polyurethane glue,
Watco Danish oil, connector bolts, hard-
ware, tools, and woodworking supplies*

WOODWORKERS SUPPLY
1108 North Glen Rd.
Casper, WY 82601
(800) 645-9292
*Veneer edge tape, shelf standards, shelf
pins, gold-leaf products, hardware, tools,
and woodworking supplies*

METRIC CONVERSION CHART

INCHES	CENTIMETERS	MILLIMETERS	INCHES	CENTIMETERS	MILLIMETERS
⅛	0.3	3	13	33.0	330
¼	0.6	6	14	35.6	356
⅜	1.0	10	15	38.1	381
½	1.3	13	16	40.6	406
⅝	1.6	16	17	43.2	432
¾	1.9	19	18	45.7	457
⅞	2.2	22	19	48.3	483
1	2.5	25	20	50.8	508
1¼	3.2	32	21	53.3	533
1½	3.8	38	22	55.9	559
1¾	4.4	44	23	58.4	584
2	5.1	51	24	61.0	610
2½	6.4	64	25	63.5	635
3	7.6	76	26	66.0	660
3½	8.9	89	27	68.6	686
4	10.2	102	28	71.1	711
4½	11.4	114	29	73.7	737
5	12.7	127	30	76.2	762
6	15.2	152	31	78.7	787
7	17.8	178	32	81.3	813
8	20.3	203	33	83.8	838
9	22.9	229	34	86.4	864
10	25.4	254	35	88.9	889
11	27.9	279	36	91.4	914
12	30.5	305			

INDEX

INDEX